COMPANION TO
THE BOOK OF SERVICES

COMPANION TO THE BOOK OF SERVICES

Introduction, Commentary, and Instructions for Using the New United Methodist Services

SUPPLEMENTAL WORSHIP RESOURCES 17

Abingdon Press
Nashville

COMPANION TO *THE BOOK OF SERVICES*

Copyright © 1988 by Abingdon Press

This book is printed on acid-free paper.

Library of Congress Cataloging-in-Publication Data

Companion to The Book of services: introduction, commentary, and instructions for using the new United Methodist services.
p. cm.—(Supplemental worship resources: 17)
Bibliography: p.
ISBN 0-687-09257-4 (pbk.: alk. paper)
1. United Methodist Church (U.S.). Book of services. 2. United Methodist Church (U.S.)—Liturgy. 3. Methodist Church—Liturgy. I. United Methodist Church (U.S.). Book of services. II. Series.
BX8337.U54 1985 Suppl.
264'.076—dc19   87-28409
                                                                      CIP

Scripture quotations are from the New English Bible. © The Delegates of the Oxford University Press and the Syndics of the Cambridge University Press, 1961, 1970. Reprinted by permission.

MANUFACTURED BY THE PARTHENON PRESS AT
NASHVILLE, TENNESSEE, UNITED STATES OF AMERICA

Contents

The Story of
the New Services

A. The Need for United Methodist Services

The publication of *The Book of Services* in 1985, following the adoption of these services into the Ritual of The United Methodist Church by the 1984 General Conference, provided for the first time a set of official services developed by The United Methodist Church.

When The United Methodist Church was formed in 1968, both The Methodist Church and The Evangelical United Brethren Church had recently revised their rituals. The new denomination was plainly not ready for a single United Methodist ritual. And so, *The Book of Discipline* 1968 (Par. 1388) provided that "the Ritual of the Church is that contained in the *Book of Ritual* of The Evangelical United Brethren Church, 1959, and *The Book of Worship for Church and Home* of The Methodist Church."

The 1968 General Conference also set up a Commission on Worship, two of whose functions were: "3. When need arises, to prepare forms of worship and to revise existing orders of worship for recommendation to the General Conference. 4. To supervise future editions of *The Book of Worship for Church and Home*, as may be authorized by the General Conference" (*The Book of Discipline* 1968, Par. 1385).

The Commission on Worship began immediately in 1968 to develop a long-range plan. No hasty actions would be taken, since there was plenty of time before the new denomination would be

9

ready for a single ritual. There was the opportunity to do consulting, research, and testing on an unprecedented scale.

The first step was to consult as widely as possible among United Methodists to discover both what was happening in local churches and what United Methodists wanted. This was done in two ways.

(1) The Commission advertised through all available channels for local pastors and others to send in acts and services of worship that they had discovered or created and considered worth sharing. Many hundreds of responses were received, and the best of these were published in *Ventures in Worship* I (1969), II (1970), and III (1973) and *Ventures in Song* (1972).

(2) The Commission held a national convocation on worship in 1969 at Saint Louis. The convocation leadership represented a wide diversity of viewpoint and practice, and almost two thousand persons attended. Listening to the church was a major purpose of the convocation. This was done by means of open discussions at the convocation, use of an evaluation instrument, and encouragement of further responses both during and after the convocation.

As the Commission listened to all these United Methodists, several things became evident. (1) Many United Methodists wished to continue using the existing Methodist and Evangelical United Brethren rituals, and the Commission was confirmed in its judgment that these should not be hastily replaced (2) Many others enjoyed the freedom to be creative or to follow local or ethnic customs, and they should be encouraged. (3) A large and growing group of United Methodists was asking for a carefully developed new ritual and orders of worship that they could have a part in testing.

Many in this last group were aware of the amazing renewal of worship that was already taking place in many Christian denominations. This renewal had its roots in movements that had been gaining momentum in both Protestant and Catholic circles for many years. By 1970, trial or official liturgies reflecting this renewal were beginning to appear in other denominations. What was especially astonishing was the way in which the liturgies of diverse Christian denominations were converging toward common patterns that reflected both our knowledge of biblical and early church worship and the needs and experiences of Christians today. Could The United Methodist Church develop services that reflected this ecumenical Christian renewal, while at the same time keeping what is distinctive in our denominational heritage and enjoying our historic liturgical freedoms?

B. Developing Supplemental Worship Resources

The Commission on Worship responded first with a pilot project. Work was begun in 1970 on a service text for the proclamation of the Word and the celebration of the Lord's Supper. A Committee on Alternate Rituals was set up (see p. 22), and consultants were brought in to work with it. Dr. H. Grady Hardin was elected to chair the committee, and Dr. James F. White was elected writer of the text. Both were then professors at Perkins School of Theology. Through the cooperative work of this committee and of the Commission as a whole, the text went through eight drafts before being approved for publication in leaflet form as *The Sacrament of the Lord's Supper: An Alternate Text 1972*. It appeared just in time to be used as the opening service of Holy Communion at the 1972 General Conference, and after an extremely favorable reception there it went on during the next eight years to sell more than two million copies.

That General Conference also merged the Commission on Worship with several other agencies to form the General Board of Discipleship and authorized it not only to continue the functions of the Commission on Worship, but also "to prepare new and alternate rituals and orders of worship" (*The Book of Discipline* 1972, Par. 1023.4). This authorization was continued in the 1976 *Discipline* (Par. 1316.5).

The General Board of Discipleship established a Section on Worship and Theology, to which these functions were assigned, and the Section began work in 1973 on (1) baptism and confirmation; (2) new orders and services of Sunday worship, with and without Holy Communion; (3) weddings; and (4) funerals and memorial services.

A procedure was developed whereby each of these projects was assigned to a research and writing task force. Each task force was asked to prepare a draft for a paperback book or booklet containing not only proposed text, but also introduction, commentary, and additional resources as needed to help pastors use the service. Drafts were submitted to the entire elected membership of the Section on Worship, serving as the Editorial Committee. This Editorial Committee was chaired by H. Grady Hardin (1972–1976) and James F. White (1976–1980). The Section could approve or disapprove, amend, or send drafts back to the task force for rewriting. Task force and Section members were often able to give texts trial use in local churches while they were still in preliminary draft. Section members took much time and great interest in perfecting these drafts, which were usually sent back several times to the task force for revision or rewriting. The Section worked closely with The United Methodist Publishing House, and when the Section was convinced that a manuscript was ready for widespread testing and unofficial use, it was approved and submitted for publication.

The resulting series of publications was at first referred to as the "Alternate Rituals" Series, but when that title proved to be confusing, the series was renamed the "Supplemental Worship Resources" (SWR) Series.

The Sacrament of the Lord's Supper: An Alternate Text 1972, already in print, was listed as Supplemental Worship Resources (SWR) 1. A contest was held by the Section and by Abingdon Press for the best musical setting of this service, and the winner was the Rev. Richard L. Fleming, Minister of Music at First United Methodist Church, Richardson, Texas. His musical setting was published in *The Sacrament of the Lord's Supper: An Alternate Text (Music Edition)* in 1975. A Spanish language version entitled *El Sacramento de la Santa Cena* was prepared by Ms. Theresa Santillan and the Rev. Dr. Roberto Escamilla of the Board of Discipleship staff and published in 1978.

SWR 2, published in 1976, is *A Service of Baptism, Confirmation, and Renewal*. It was drafted by a task force chaired by Professor Laurence Hull Stookey of Wesley Theological Seminary, who also served as writer. Other task force members were the Rev. Richard F. Collman (pastor of the Headwaters Parish in Minnesota), the Rev. Chester E. Custer and the Rev. Hoyt L. Hickman of the Board of Discipleship staff, and Professor Lawrence Wagley of Saint Paul School of Theology.

SWR 3, also published in 1976, is *Word and Table: A Basic*

Pattern of Sunday Worship for United Methodists. It was drafted by a task force chaired by Professor Don E. Saliers of Emory University, who also served as writer. Other task force members were Professor Julian Hartt of the University of Virginia, James F. White, and Hoyt L. Hickman.

Although *Word and Table* included a calendar and lectionary, it soon became evident that more comprehensive resources were needed in this area. In 1977, the *Word and Table* task force (except for Julian Hartt, who had retired) was reconvened. This resulted in the publication of *Seasons of the Gospel* (SWR 6—James F. White, writer), *From Ashes to Fire* (SWR 8—Don E. Saliers, writer) in 1979, and *From Hope to Joy* (SWR 15—Don E. Saliers, writer) in 1984.

SWR 5, published in 1979, is *A Service of Christian Marriage.* It was drafted by a task force chaired by the Rev. Robert E. Scoggin, Minister of Music at Christ United Methodist Church in Rochester, Minnesota. The Rev. Dr. M. Lawrence Snow, Pastor of the Community United Methodist Church in Poughkeepsie, New York, was the principal writer. The Rev. Sharon Neufer Emswiler and the Rev. Thomas Neufer Emswiler, co-directors of the Wesley Foundation in Normal, Illinois, assisted in the writing. Other members of the task force were the Rev. Dr. L. L. Haynes, Jr. (Pastor of Wesley United Methodist Church in Baton Rouge, Louisiana), the Rev. Douglass J. McKee (Associate Pastor of the First United Methodist Church in Cheyenne, Wyoming), and Hoyt L. Hickman. The Rev. Thom C. Jones of the Board of Discipleship staff and the Rev. Dr. Carlton R. Young of Emory University assisted in the preparation of musical suggestions. Dr. Ekkehard Muehlenberg of Claremont School of Theology served as consultant.

SWR 7, published in 1979, is *A Service of Death and Resurrection: The Ministry of the Church at Death.* It was drafted by a task force chaired by Professor Emeritus Paul W. Hoon of Union Theological Seminary, who was also the principal writer. Other members of the task force were the Rev. Dr. William K. Burns (Minister of Music at Morrow Memorial United Methodist Church in Maplewood, New Jersey), the Rev. Dr. L. L. Haynes, Jr., Hoyt L. Hickman, and the Rev. Dr. Edgar N. Jackson (retired minister of the New York Conference, author, and lecturer).

Thom C. Jones and Dr. Carlton R. Young assisted in the preparation of musical suggestions. Dr. Ekkehard Muehlenberg served as consultant, and Dr. Peggy West of United Methodist Communications edited parts of the manuscript.

All these services were published with the invitation for those who used them to give their evaluation and suggestions, and as a result a wealth of helpful suggestions was received. These services were also reviewed and in many cases used by liturgical scholars, pastors, and congregations of other denominations; suggestions from their perspectives were most helpful.

In the light of all these suggestions, the Word and Table; Baptism, Confirmation, and Renewal; Christian Marriage; and Death and Resurrection service texts were revised under the editorship of James F. White and published early in 1980 in the booklet *We Gather Together* (SWR 10). These revised services were submitted to the 1980 General Conference, which commended them to local churches for trial use and instructed the General Board of Discipleship to revise these services in the light of this trial use and to submit them to the 1984 General Conference for adoption into the Ritual of the Church.

Following this action, several additional resources incorporating these revised texts were published. Revised editions of SWR 1, 2, and 3 were edited by Hoyt L. Hickman in consultation with the original writers and published in 1980 and 1981. The SWR books published in 1979 were judged not to need revision. *Word and Table* (SWR 3) was translated and adapted by Roberto Escamilla and a large group of Hispanic consultants and published in 1981 as *Palabra y Sacramento. We Gather Together* (SWR 10) was translated and adapted by Theresa Santillan with the assistance of Roberto Escamilla and published in 1981 as *Congregados in Su Nombre. English-Japanese Parallel: A Sunday Service*, a translation and adaptation of the first part of *We Gather Together*, was prepared by a committee consisting of the Rev. Jonathan Fujita (Centenary United Methodist Church in Los Angeles), the Rev. Nobuaki Hanaoka (Pine United Methodist Church in San Francisco), the Rev. Hidemi Ito (Simpson United Methodist Church in Arvada, Colorado), and the Rev. Frank Yoshio Ohtomo (Wesley United Methodist Church in San Jose) and published by Discipleship Resources in 1982. Development of *At the Lord's Table: A Communion Service Book for Use by the Minister* (SWR 9), based on the revised Lord's Supper text, had been authorized when the *Word and Table* task force was reconstituted in 1977. It was prepared by Hoyt L. Hickman in consultation with the other members of that task force and published in 1981.

The 1980 General Conference also adopted into the Ritual of the Church new services for the ordination of deacons and elders and the consecration of bishops, as official alternatives to the services inherited from the Methodist and Evangelical United Brethren Churches. Because of the historic and disciplinary roles of the bishops and of the General Board of Higher Education and Ministry in ordinations and consecrations, these services had been developed by a process different from that described above. The 1976 General Conference, in addition to continuing the functions in the area of worship given to the General Board of Discipleship, had taken actions relating to the ordained ministry and to inclusive language, which called for revised ordination and consecration services. In response, the Council of Bishops voted in 1977 to set up a Committee to Study the Ordinal and invited the Board of Higher Education and Ministry and the General Board of Discipleship to join them in naming members to this committee. When this committee organized and began its work, it determined that, given the nature of ordination and consecration, it was inappropriate to publish unofficial trial ordination and consecration services comparable to the other service texts in the SWR Series. Instead, the committee developed an introduction and texts, entitled *An Ordinal*, which was submitted with a petition by the General Board of Discipleship to the 1980 General Conference for its adoption as part of the official Ritual of The United Methodist Church.

An Ordinal was officially adopted by the 1980 General Conference and shortly afterward published as a separate book by The United Methodist Publishing House under the same title. The complete story of its development, including the names of all the persons involved, can be found there. Because ordination and consecration services are conducted by bishops at annual and jurisdictional conferences, using custom-printed bulletins, they are not included in *The Book of Services,* which is designed for the use of ministers and local churches.

Meanwhile, other SWR volumes were being developed for purposes *other than* testing texts for possible submission to General Conference as proposed official ritual. While they are unrelated to *The Book of Services* and to this book, a mention of them here will indicate the scope of the SWR Series as a whole. *Ritual in a New Day: An Invitation* (SWR 4, 1976) continued the work of the previous Ventures series by reporting on experimental acts of worship taking place in local churches. Following authorization by the 1976 General Conference, *Supplement to the Book of Hymns* (SWR 11, 1982), *Songs of Zion* (SWR 12, 1981), *Hymns from the Four Winds* (SWR 13, 1983), and *Celebremos* I and II (published by Discipleship Resources in 1979 and 1983) supplemented existing hymnals and also tested hymns and songs for possible inclusion in the next official hymnal. *Blessings and Consecrations: A Book of Occasional Services* (SWR 14, 1984) provided an updated and expanded alternative to Part IV of *The Book of Worship for Church and Home.*

C. The New Services Become Official

During the period of official trial use from 1980 to 1984, the proposed new United Methodist services were subjected to intense scrutiny. In 1980, the Section on Worship elected Hoyt L. Hickman editor of these services and continued, both by mail and at meetings, to perfect them. Another large quantity of helpful criticism and suggestions was received from local churches and from expert reviews, both in our denomination and ecumenically. Proposed changes in the services were reviewed by outside consultants. Of these, Paul W. Hoon, Don E. Saliers, M. Lawrence Snow, Laurence Hull Stookey, and James F. White had been key members of the original writing task forces. The Rev. Dr. William H. Willimon, then pastor of the Northside United Methodist Church in Greenville, South Carolina, was also helpful. Ecumenical perspective was added by Dr. Gail Ramshaw-Schmidt (Lutheran) and Ms. Susan J. White (Episcopal).

Special care was taken to test the suitability of these services in ethnic minority local churches. A consultation with selected black pastors was followed by the trial use of these services in their congregations and a second consultation in which they gave their evaluations and suggestions, which were most helpful. In the light of the trial use of *Congregados en Su Nombre,* a Spanish language version of these services with Hispanic cultural adaptations was prepared by the Rev. Hugo Lopez of the Board of Discipleship staff with the aid of Hispanic consultants, and there was fruitful interchange between those working on the Spanish and English versions. A Korean version with cultural adaptations was developed by the Rev. Sang E. Chun of the General Board of Discipleship staff with the aid of Korean consultants, but there was inadequate time for testing in local churches, and as a result it was not submitted to the 1984 General Conference.

When the revision of the services in English and Spanish was completed, the General Board of Discipleship submitted these services to the 1984 General Conference for adoption. The texts, with a general preface and with introductions concerning each service, were printed in full in both languages in the Advance Edition of *The Daily Christian Advocate* (pages E88-E138), so that delegates would have ample time to study them prior to General Conference. A related petition from the Board asked that the Ritual be redefined in *The Book of Discipline* to include these new services.

At the 1984 General Conference, these services were extensively discussed in the legislative Committee on Discipleship. Only one amendment was made there, adding "(UNITED METHODIST KINGDOMTIDE)" after "SEASON AFTER PENTECOST" in the Calendar. The Committee then approved the petition to adopt these services by a vote of 102 in favor, none against, and one abstention (*Daily Christian Advocate,* 382). This vote would have placed it on the General Conference consent calendar, but it was wisely taken off that calendar so that it could be considered separately by the whole General Conference.

The full General Conference then overwhelmingly voted its approval (*DCA,* 799-800) by a show of hands, with only a few scattered negative votes. Not only were these services adopted, but also the definition of the Ritual in *The Book of Discipline* (Par.

1214.3) was changed to read: "The Ritual of the Church is that contained in the Book of Ritual of The Evangelical United Brethren Church, 1959, 'The General Services of the Church' in The Book of Worship for Church and Home of The Methodist Church, The Ordinal 1981, and 'The General Services of the Church 1984' (English and Spanish versions)."

"The General Services of the Church 1984" in English, including the preface and introductions, which had also been approved by General Conference, was published by The United Methodist Publishing House in November 1985 as *The Book of Services*. The title reflects the fact that this book—like *The Book of Worship for Church and Home, The Book of Hymns, The Book of Discipline,* and *The Book of Resolutions*—is an official book of The United Methodist Church. To the best of our knowledge, the only similar title ever given to a book by any of the predecessors of The United Methodist Church was the *Book of Service*, publishd by The Methodist Episcopal Church in 1932, immediately following the adoption by its General Conference of the new official ritual and orders of worship.

By agreement between The United Methodist Publishing House and Discipleship Resources (a publishing unit of the General Board of Discipleship), "The General Services of the Church 1984" in Spanish, with preface and introductions, was published by Discipleship Resources in January 1985 as *Cultos Principales de la Iglesia.* This book was a double "first." While previous ritual in English had been translated into Spanish, this was the first official Spanish language ritual in the history of The United Methodist Church and its predecessors to be directly adopted by General Conference. It was also the first time in our denominational history that such a book had been published in Spanish *before* its equivalent was published in English.

The General Board of Discipleship is keenly aware of the need for these services, with appropriate cultural adaptations, to be published in other languages. Work is proceeding toward this end.

D. Basic Understandings

Four basic understandings were spelled out in the preface to the General Services, which the delegates had before them as they deliberated and voted. These understandings are crucial in perceiving the intent of the General Conference in adopting these services. For that reason, they are repeated below exactly as the Section on Worship and the General Board of Discipleship submitted them, as General Conference approved them, and as they appear in the Preface to *The Book of Services.*

1. Adoption of these General Services into the Ritual of the Church in no way takes away the status of the existing Ritual of the Church (Methodist and Evangelical United Brethren) or discourages its use. Rather, by giving all three sets of General Services a place in the Ritual of the Church, a wide choice is being offered the congregations of our diverse denomination.

2. The various General Services are designed for maximum flexibility, so that with appropriate adaptations they can be used in a variety of situations. United Methodist local churches range from very large to very small in membership, from very formal to very informal in worship style, from print oriented to orally oriented, and with a wide variety of ethnic and cultural heritages. Even so, there will be situations where adaptations are called for in a particular situation that are not explicitly provided for in the services themselves. In such cases it is hoped that those planning and leading worship will know that they have Christian liberty to meet the pastoral needs of their congregations.

3. Inevitably these services contain compromises at points where United Methodists are not of one mind. One especially difficult area throughout the years during which these services have been developed has been that of the tension between traditional and inclusive language. It has been the basic intention throughout the development process to avoid language that discriminates against women, against any racial or ethnic community, or against persons with handicapping conditions. Two particular guiding principles in this connection have been (a) not to use masculine language to refer to people in general, and (b) to seek a balanced diversity of scriptural imagery in addressing or referring to God. In practice, however, there have been frequent disagreements about particular usages. Many active participants in the development process would have preferred wording different from that which now appears. These services as they stand represent the best resolution possible at this time. Those using these services may from time to time wish to change particular

words deemed objectionable, and they should be assured of their freedom to do so.

4. This diversity should not obscure our fundamental unity in Christ and in historic Christianity. We stand on the fourfold authority of Scripture, tradition, experience, and reason—with Scripture primary. These services seek to avoid anything faddish or idiosyncratic. They represent an earnest attempt to heed Wesley's admonition that our worship "follow the Scriptures and the primitive Church," while at the same time speaking to the condition of contemporary United Methodists. They represent an attempt to incorporate both the historic and ecumenical witness of the church and also the distinctive gifts that our United Methodist heritage enables us to contribute to the universal church. (pp. 7-9)

E. Completion of the SWR Series

There remained the task of combining and revising earlier SWR publications into books that would provide the necessary assistance to those who use the new services.

In 1983 it was agreed that *Seasons of the Gospel* (SWR 6), *From Ashes to Fire* (SWR 8), and *From Hope to Joy* (SWR 15) should be revised and combined into a single book of resources for the entire Christian year, based on the Common Calendar and Lectionary. Since such a book would serve other denominations using the Common Calendar and Lectionary as well as United Methodists, it was agreed that this should be an Abingdon Press trade book and not an SWR book. The writers selected were Hoyt L. Hickman (who also served as general editor), Laurence Hull Stookey, Don E. Saliers, and James F. White. The result was *Handbook of the Christian Year*, published in 1986.

A communion service book for use by the minister was needed to supplement *The Book of Services* in the same way that *At the Lord's Table* (SWR 9) supplemented *We Gather Together* (SWR 10). Hoyt L. Hickman was named writer and editor. Consultants included the members of the *Word and Table* task force: Ms. Barbara P. Garcia, Thomas A. Langford III, and Michael Williams of the General Board of Discipleship staff; and Laurence Hull Stookey. The result was *Holy Communion: A*

Communion Service Book for Use by the Minister (SWR 16), published in 1987.

Companion to the Book of Services (SWR 17) is the final volume projected for the SWR series. It is a revision of *Baptism, Confirmation, and Renewal* (SWR 2); *Word and Table* (SWR 3); *A Service of Christian Marriage* (SWR 5); and *A Service of Death and Resurrection* (SWR 7). It combines them into one volume designed to be, as its name implies, a companion to *The Book of Services*, not only for pastors and other leaders of worship, but also for all who wish to understand better these services. Like other publications in the SWR series, it represents the work of many persons. The Section on Worship determined the specifications of the book and gave their approval and sponsorship to its publication. Hoyt L. Hickman was the general editor and the writer of the material not taken from the earlier volumes in this series. The writers of the predecessor books (Laurence Hull Stookey, Don E. Saliers, James F. White, M. Lawrence Snow, and Paul W. Hoon) and the other staff of the Section on Worship (Thomas A. Langford III, Diana Sanchez, and Michael Williams) served as consultants and made many helpful suggestions.

The members and staff of the Section on Worship wish to thank the persons named above and the many others who have shared with us ideas that have contributed to this book and to the other books in the SWR series. We are confident that our predecessors on the General Board of Discipleship and the Commission on Worship would join us in this expression of thanks. Although this series is ending, we are committed to produce further resources as they are needed in the future. Reactions and suggestions are welcomed by the Section on Worship, P. O. Box 840, Nashville, Tennessee 37202-0840.

May this book, and the services which it accompanies, be used to the glory of God and the proclamation of the gospel of Jesus Christ.

Commission on Worship 1968–72

*Bishop Lance Webb, Chairman
*William F. Dunkle, Jr., Vice-chairman

*Hoyt L. Hickman, Executive Secretary
*Marvin A. Schilling, Treasurer
*J. Robert Hammond
*H. Grady Hardin
Emory S. Bucke
Paul M. Davis
Eugene T. Drinkhard
Edith Farrar
Joe A. Harding
Gertrude Harrell
Bishop Paul M. Herrick
Eugene C. Holmes
J. D. Killingsworth
Mary K. Longstreth
Chilton C. McPheeters
Patti H. Rankin 1970–72
Kenneth Robinson
Member of the Executive Committee

Committee on Alternate Rituals 1970–72

H. Grady Hardin, Chairperson
Emory S. Bucke
David G. Buttrick, Consultant
William F. Dunkle, Jr.
Edith Farrar
Benjamin Garrison, Consultant
Fred D. Gealy, Consultant
J. Robert Hammond
Hoyt L. Hickman
Eugene C. Holmes
David J. Randolph, Jr., Staff, Board of Evangelism
Marvin A. Schilling
Lawrence Hull Stookey, Consultant
Bishop Lance Webb
James F. White, Writer and Consultant

General Board of Discipleship
Members of the Area on Worship 1972–75
(Included the Section on Worship and Theology
and The Upper Room)

Eugene C. Holmes, Chairperson
Louise H. Shown, Secretary
Paul F. Abel
Phyllis Close
Grace Etcheto
H. Grady Hardin
L. L. Haynes, Jr.
Patti Rankin
Robert Scoggin
Paul Shepherd
Laurence Hull Stookey
Bishop Edward L. Tullis

General Board of Discipleship
Members of the Section on Worship 1975–76

Eugene C. Holmes, Chairperson
Louise H. Shown, Secretary
Rosalie Bentzinger
Phyllis Close
Grace Etcheto
H. Grady Hardin
L. L. Haynes, Jr.
Patti Rankin
Robert Scoggin
Laurence Hull Stookey
Bishop John Warman

General Board of Discipleship
Members of the Section on Worship 1976–80

*Bishop Robert E. Goodrich, Jr., Chairperson 1976–78
*Louise H. Shown, Vice-chairperson 1976–78,
Chairperson 1978–80

*Paul F. Abel, Vice-chairperson 1978–80
*L. Doyle Masters, Secretary (Deceased January 27, 1980)
Phyllis Close
Edward L. Duncan
Judy Gilreath
Kay Hereford
*Judith Kelsey-Powell
Marilynn Mabee
William B. McClain
*James F. White
*Carlton R. Young
Philip E. Baker, Representing the Fellowship of U. M. Musicians
Elise M. Shoemaker, Representing the U. M.
Society for Worship 1977–78
Pat Crotty, Representing the U. M. Society for Worship 1978–80
*Members of the Executive Editorial Committee

General Board of Discipleship
Members of the Section on Worship 1980–84

Stanley P. DePano, Chairperson
George W. Watson, Sr., Vice-chairperson
D. S. Dharmapalan, Secretary
Bishop George W. Bashore
Donald Bueg
Carole Cotton-Winn
Melissa Lynn Ives
J. Sue Kana-Mackey
Merwin Kurtz
Cindy Locklear 1980–82
Mary Penn
Luis Sotomayor
Sharon Spieth
Langill Watson 1982–84
Janet Lee and Patty Evans, Representing the Fellowship of
United Methodists in Worship, Music and Other Arts 1980–83
Robert Bennett and Jerry Henry, Representing
the Fellowship 1983–84

General Board of Discipleship
Members of the Section on Worship 1984–88

Stanley P. DePano, Chairperson
Nancy Brady, Vice-chairperson
Gloster Current, Secretary
Bruce Blake
Carole Cotton-Winn
D. S. Dharmapalan
Margarida Fortunato
Samuel Kaiser
J. Sue Kana-Mackey
Ruth Thomasson
Bishop Walter Underwood
Robert Bennett and Jerry Henry, Representing the Fellowship
Michael O'Donnell, Representing the Order of Saint Luke

General Board of Discipleship
General Secretaries

Melvin G. Talbert, 1973–80
Haviland Houston (acting), 1980–81
Ezra Earl Jones, 1981—

Associate General Secretaries Relating to Worship

Ira Gallaway, 1972–74
Rueben Job, 1974–77
Roberto Escamilla, 1977–80
Noe E. Gonzales, 1982–86
Alan Waltz, 1985—

Assistant General Secretaries, Section on Worship

David J. Randolph, 1972–74
Roberto Escamilla, 1974–77 (acting 1977–78)

Hoyt L. Hickman, 1978–85
Thomas A. Langford III, 1985–

Other Section on Worship Staff

Hoyt L. Hickman, 1972–78, 1985—
Chester E. Custer, 1972–73
Thom C. Jones, 1974–78
Richard L. Eslinger, 1978–83
Elise M. Shoemaker, 1978–81
Barbara P. Garcia, 1980–85
Judy L. Loehr, 1981–85
Michael Williams, 1984—
Diana Sanchez, 1986—

CHAPTER I

Services of Word and Table

A. Introduction to the Services

1. One Basic Pattern

United Methodists, along with many in other traditions within the Christian family of faith, are in the midst of the reform and renewal of worship. The action of the 1984 General Conference in officially adopting these Services of Word and Table is a key event in this renewal. This is part of our ongoing struggle to be a more faithful and vital church.

However, the reform and renewal of our worship is not simply a matter of producing a new liturgy and new forms and materials for worship. It is nothing less than the recovery of Christ in the life of the church and its mission in the world. This renewal will fail if those who use these approved services follow the letter without the Spirit.

Central to the renewal of our worship is the renewal of the regular Sunday worship in each local church. For this reason, *The Book of Services* begins with "Services of Word and Table"—in other words, the Sunday Service. Denominational service books have sometimes begun with the calendar or with daily worship or with baptism, and good reasons can be given for beginning with any of these. Nevertheless, because the most basic day in the calendar is the Lord's Day (Sunday), and because Sunday worship is where we establish and renew our identity as a community of faith, we start with what happens on the Lord's

Day. As we shall see, baptism and other services of the baptismal covenant normally occur in the context of the Sunday Service, and both the Service of Christian Marriage and the Service of Death and Resurrection follow the same basic pattern as does the Sunday Service.

A basic pattern of worship for the proclamation of God's Word and the celebration of the Lord's Supper is presented in *The Book of Services*. It is designed to express the biblical, historical, and theological bases that give integrity to Christian worship. It is printed in several formats to show how it can be adapted to differing situations. It is a pattern from which can emerge a variety of developing orders and texts beyond the particular ones printed in *The Book of Services*. It reflects the fact that we are a church with a common faith, but with diverse ways of expressing this faith in worship.

This basic pattern and related orders of worship seek to incorporate the insights that have emerged during a period of great sharing among many Christian traditions. We have been moving beyond simply revising the patterns of our recent past. We have rediscovered the roots of our own denominational worship heritage and the liturgies of the Reformation. As United Methodists, we are heirs of the Wesleys' Anglicanism, of the diverse influences that shaped Asbury, of Albright's Lutheran heritage, of Otterbein's Reformed heritage, of the Anabaptist heritage of Boehm and Newcomer, and of the American experience that shaped Methodists and Evangelicals and United Brethren alike. We have gone behind these to an even broader, more inclusive heritage from the early church as well. Beside the text of John Wesley's 1784 *Sunday Service of the Methodists in North America*, based on *The Book of Common Prayer* of The Church of England, are the words of the letter he sent with that service: "They [the American Methodists] are now at full liberty, simply to follow the scriptures and the primitive church. And we judge it best that they should stand fast in that liberty, wherewith God has so strangely made them free."[1]

The structure and unfolding rhythm of the Services of Word and Table clearly show the influence of some of the earliest worship patterns and texts in the Christian community. The unified service, with its twofold division of the Service of the

Word and the Service of the Thanksgiving Meal, reflects early practices. The restoration of the ancient emphasis on the reading and preaching of scripture, on congregational prayer, on praise and thanksgiving, on the sign actions of the bread and cup, and on the role of the Holy Spirit in the worship of God's people brings forth new theological understandings. In its basics, the pattern in these Services of Word and Table is far older than the more recent patterns to which we may be accustomed.

2. Biblical Roots

The pattern and content of these services are rooted in worship as Jesus and his earliest disciples knew it—the services in the synagogue and the family worship that centered around the table.

The first part of these services of Word and Table, the Service of the Word, has its origins in the synagogue. We are not sure just how and when synagogue worship originated, but it may have been in the sixth century before Christ, when large numbers of Jews had been taken from their native land and found themselves in exile in Babylon. The Temple in Jerusalem had been destroyed. The Jews asked, "How shall we sing the Lord's song in a foreign land?" (Psalm 137:4). They began to hold gatherings or assemblies where there were readings from the scriptures and teaching based on these readings. Interspersed were praises to God, probably including the psalms. The term *synagogue*, which literally means gathering or assembly, was applied first to these assemblies and later also to the houses built to accommodate these assemblies. Even after the Temple in Jerusalem was rebuilt, most Jews could go there only occasionally, if at all, and ordinarily worshiped in the synagogue where they lived.

Jesus began his public ministry preaching and teaching in synagogues. In his home town of Nazareth, for instance, "he went to the synagogue, as his custom was, on the sabbath day." He read Isaiah 61:1-2 from the scriptures and then preached to those assembled (Luke 4:16 ff.). The Christian Service of the Word today is essentially a slightly amplified version of this synagogue pattern.

The second part of these services of Word and Table is rooted in Jewish family worship. As Jesus and his disciples traveled together, they also ate together, and as devout Jews they considered these meals sacred occasions to be observed with thanksgiving to God. The family meal table had long been the center of Jewish family worship. Jesus and his disciples, having left their families to travel together, had themselves become a family.

Jesus' supper with his disciples on the night before his death was both the last of these meals and the beginning of a transformed meal that Christians have eaten ever since. That night Jesus added something new to the sacred family meal they had known. As he gave them the bread he said, "This is my body. . . . Do this in remembrance of me." As he gave them the cup of wine he said, "This is my blood. . . . Do this, as often as you drink it, in remembrance of me" (Matthew 26:26 ff., Mark 14:22, Luke 22:19-20, I Corinthians 11:23 ff.). Actually, the word we translate "remember" might better be translated "recall" in the sense of "call back": "Do this to call me back."

When Jesus was killed, his disciples were scattered, but two days later on the first Easter they found themselves face-to-face with the living, risen Christ. They found faith and meaning for their lives and a message for the world. Ever since, Christians have been an Easter people. Luke's Gospel (chapter 24) describes the encounter of the disciples with the living Christ in a way that suggests a transformed synagogue service and a transformed holy meal. When the two disciples walking from Jerusalem to Emmaus had been joined by Jesus and had poured out their hearts to him, he quoted to them extensively from "Moses and all the prophets" (major sections of the scriptures that Christians call the Old Testament) and *interpreted* these scriptures to them, a term that to Luke's readers would indicate what was done in the synagogue and its Christian equivalent. When they got to Emmaus and sat down to their evening meal, Jesus began to do what he had done before at such meals. "He took the bread and blessed, and broke it, and gave it to them. And their eyes were opened and they recognized him. . . . He was known to them in the breaking of the bread" (Luke 24:30, 35). Later that evening in Jerusalem, he appeared to a larger group of disciples, ate in their presence, and "opened their minds to understand the scriptures" (v. 45).

John's Gospel (chapters 20-21) tells not only how the risen

Christ ate breakfast with his disciples, but also how Thomas, when he encountered the risen Christ, said, "My Lord and my God!" Ever since, Christians have seen encounters with the risen Christ as encounters with God.

We read that Jesus then ascended into heaven, is at the right hand of God, and "fills all in all" (Acts 1:9-11; Ephesians 1:20-23). He promised his disciples, "I am with you always" (Matthew 28:20). In other words, just as God is everywhere and can be encountered and worshiped anywhere, so also can the risen and ascended Christ.

Furthermore, Christ promised at his ascension, "You shall receive power when the Holy Spirit has come upon you"; and this happened on the day of Pentecost (Acts 2). From that day to this, Christian worship has been an encounter with the living God through the risen Christ in the power of the Holy Spirit. This is one way of defining Christian worship.

After the disciples went out preaching and teaching with the power of the Holy Spirit on the day of Pentecost, they continued to take part in synagogue worship wherever they went (Acts 9:2, 9:20, 13:5, 13:13 ff., 13:44 ff., 14:1, 17:1 ff., 17:10 ff., 17:17 ff., 18:4, 18:19, 18:26, 19:8, 22:19, 24:12, 26:11) and to break bread as a holy meal in their own gatherings (Acts 2:42, 2:46). Their preaching and teaching about Jesus led eventually to a break between church and synagogue, and the Christians held their own adaptation of the synagogue service when they gathered on the first day of the week for "the breaking of bread." Interspersed with reading and preaching the Word of God, these Christians would, we gather, "sing psalms and hymns and spiritual songs with thankfulness . . . to God" (Colossians 3:16). This adapted synagogue service became the first part of the combined service and came to be called the *synaxis*—a word that, like *synagogue*, means "gathering." Such a combined service of Word and Table is described in Acts 20:7 ff.

3. Historical Development

About A.D 155, Justin Martyr, writing in his *First Apology* to pagans to correct vicious rumors about what Christians did when they gathered for worship, gave this description of Christian Sunday worship:

> And on the day called Sunday there is a meeting in one place of those who live in cities or the country, and the memoirs of the apostles [that later became the New Testament] or the writings of the prophets [Old Testament] are read as long as time permits. When the reader has finished, the presider in a discourse [sermon] urges and invites [us] to the imitation of these noble things. Then we all stand up and offer prayers. . . . When we have finished the prayer, bread is brought, and wine with water, and the presider similarly sends up prayers and thanksgivings to the best of his ability, and the congregation assents, saying the Amen; the distribution and reception of the consecrated [bread and wine] by each one takes place and they are sent to the absent by deacons.
> (chapter 67)

Since these Christians were under persecution and had to meet secretly in homes, it is likely that services were commonly held in haste and that nonessentials were omitted. This may account for the omission in this description of any reference to singing "psalms and hymns and spiritual songs," which would probably have been sung when possible. This may also account for the fact that the holy meal, originally a full meal, had been reduced to bread and wine, although this change may also have been a reaction to abuses, such as the overeating and overdrinking by some while others went hungry, as described in I Corinthians 11:17 ff.

Christianity grew, and by the fourth century it ceased to be persecuted and became the official religion of the Roman Empire. Christians could now worship openly, build church buildings, and expand their worship services to include ceremonial entrances and glorious acts of prayer and praise. Yet Sunday worship remained at its core the synagogue service in Christian form, followed by the holy meal.

Gradually, however, other things began to obscure the essentials, and abuses crept in. In western Europe, Latin continued to be the language of worship after it had ceased to be the language of the people. Preaching declined and often disappeared, although from time to time outstanding attempts were made to renew it. There was still the holy meal, but it became something done on behalf of the worshipers by the presiding priest, who was far removed from the people in buildings that made the area where the clergy functioned (the chancel) increasingly separate from where the people were gathered (the nave). Fewer and fewer people came forward to receive the bread and wine, and a church law had to be enacted, requiring Christians to receive communion at least once a year. By the fourteenth century, only the presiding priest was permitted to drink from the cup. Others could eat only the bread, which had become a wafer rather than full-fledged bread.

The Protestant Reformation of the sixteenth century attempted to reform many abuses in the church, including abuses in worship, but its success was only partial. The Roman Catholic Church rejected the proposed reforms and retained the allegiance of most Christians in western Europe. The Eastern Orthodox churches and the ancient Oriental churches, which had long since become separated from the church in western Europe, were untouched. The Protestant churches succeeded in restoring, in the language of the people, both the reading and the preaching of the scriptures and the people's singing of the psalms and other forms of song. Some Protestants also restored the freedom to pray extemporaneously rather than being limited to set prayer texts.

The attempts by the Reformation leaders to restore the fullness of the Lord's Supper, or Holy Communion, as they commonly termed the holy meal, were a mixed success. They did restore the right of laypersons to drink from the cup as well as to eat the bread. They also restored the practice that those present would partake unless there was some reason why they should not. The words used were in the language of the people, and there were earnest attempts to come to a more biblical understanding of the meaning of what was being done.

On the other hand, the majority of Protestant churches sooner or later settled into the pattern of celebrating Holy Communion only occasionally—usually quarterly or monthly—because the people, conditioned by centuries of receiving only rarely, rebelled at taking it more often. This happened in spite of Luther's and Calvin's clear teaching that Holy Communion should follow the Service of the Word every Sunday, and Calvin left record of his deep disappointment that he could not persuade the people at this point. Protestants also failed to restore to Holy Communion its original spirit of joyful celebration. It tended to be penitential and even funereal.

The next two centuries saw a mixture of renewal and deterioration in Protestant worship. Strong attempts were made to insist that at least two readings (even two whole chapters) of scripture be read and that the sermons be interpretations of scripture. Much congregational song was written and sung, including psalm settings. In some churches, elaborate choral and instrumental praise flourished. Some Protestant churches managed to celebrate Holy Communion every Sunday, although popular resistance eventually caused this practice largely to die out.

There were a number of especially strong renewal movements in the eighteenth century in Europe and in the eighteenth and early nineteenth centuries in America. In England, John Wesley (1703-1791), the founder of Methodism, placed new emphasis on reading and preaching the Word to those who were not being reached, and his brother Charles (1707-1788) wrote many popular hymns and set them to familiar and singable tunes that the people could readily pick up. In America, there were such figures as Jonathan Edwards, Francis Asbury, Philip Otterbein, Jacob Albright, and Thomas and Alexander Campbell. All stressed the preaching of scripture. The Campbells were also able to establish the celebration of the Lord's Supper every Sunday among their spiritual heirs, the Disciples of Christ, Christian Churches, and Churches of Christ.

The Wesleys also believed in Holy Communion as one of the primary means of grace and tried, unsuccessfully, to restore its celebration each Sunday. In his letter with the 1784 *Sunday Service of the Methodists in North America,* he wrote, "I also advise the elders to administer the supper of the Lord on every Lord's day."[2] His choice of terms shows the connection he saw between "the supper of the Lord" and the "Lord's Day." His sermon "The Duty of Constant Communion,"[3] published in 1787, is an eloquent statement of why "it is the duty of every Christian to receive the Lord's Supper as often as he can." In that sermon's preface "to the reader," he states: "The following discourse was written above five and fifty years ago, for the use of my pupils at

Oxford. . . . But I thank God I have not yet seen cause to alter my sentiments in any point which is therein delivered." It has been calculated from his diaries and journals that he personally received communion roughly once every five days throughout his adult life in an age when most parish churches of England practiced no more than quarterly communion.[4]

The American Methodists did not adopt weekly Holy Communion, partly because they suffered from a shortage of ordained elders and partly because the Methodist people were influenced by the prevailing Protestant practice of quarterly or monthly communion. Celebrations of Holy Communion were, however, of crucial importance in the revivals of the faith that took place in late eighteenth- and early nineteenth-century America, among both Christians in general and Methodists, Evangelicals, and United Brethren in particular.

American Methodists also found Wesley's *Sunday Service* too bound to a printed text (i.e., too "formal") for their Sunday services, and in the 1792 *Discipline* they made radical changes. The first half of the printed text of the Lord's Supper (the Service of the Word) was omitted from the printed Ritual, leaving a printed text only for the Service of the Table.[5] The Service of the Word, which became the usual Sunday service and was the first part of the service when there was Holy Communion, was no longer a printed text.

This did not mean, however, that the Sunday service was without form. In the same 1792 *Discipline*, these "directions" were "given for the establishment of uniformity in public worship among us, on the Lord's day": "1. Let the morning-service consist of singing, prayer, the reading of one chapter out of the Old Testament, and another out of the New, and preaching. . . . 4. But, on the days of administering the Lord's Supper, the two chapters in the morning-service may be omitted."[6] This, with very few changes, remained the basic pattern of nineteenth-century Methodist worship and is basic even to understanding the reforms of the twentieth century.

This is clearly a service of the Word. A large quantity of scripture is read, and the preaching of the Word follows the reading of the Word. One may assume that the preaching is to be based on the scripture that has been read.

In the generations that followed, less and less scripture was prescribed. Already permission had been given to omit the scripture readings when the Lord's Supper was administered. The reading of two "chapters" was changed to two "lessons" by the Methodist Episcopal Church in 1864[7] and by the M. E. Church South in 1870.[8] The hymnal used by both denominations beginning in 1905[9] included a psalter, but the "Order of Worship" in the front of the hymnal provided that it could be used responsively as the "lesson from the Old Testament," thus tempting Methodists to omit all but one of the Old Testament books from public reading as well as giving the impression that the psalter is for *reading* rather than for *praying and praising.* After the union of 1939, which formed The Methodist Church, the orders of worship in the hymnal simply referred to "The Lesson from the Holy Scriptures" and to "The Responsive Reading." In practice, there were many local churches in which there were neither scripture lesson nor responsive reading, except for what might (or might not) be quoted or referred to in the sermon.

By this time, there was a widespread sense that something had been lost in worship that needed to be restored. There was a trend throughout in the late nineteenth and early twentieth centuries to "enrich" forms of worship that were experienced as impoverished. Many acts of prayer and praise were added, until the simple pattern of early nineteenth-century Methodist worship had become a complex order of worship.

Unfortunately, these additions were based on the model of Morning Prayer and Sermon, which was the prevailing form of Sunday worship in Episcopal churches at the time. The basic problem with this is that Morning Prayer is a praise and prayer service, not a preaching service. It was not designed to be the main weekly service, and Wesley protested against tendencies in the Church of England during his lifetime to make it such. He included it in his 1784 *Sunday Service of the Methodists in North America,* without provision for a sermon, for occasions other than the main weekly service, or for when no ordained minister was available. The pattern of Methodist worship prescribed beginning in 1792, as we have seen, was *not* that of Morning Prayer but a Service of the Word.

During the middle years of the twentieth century, both Methodist and Evangelical United Brethren churches were commonly ordering their worship on a pattern consisting of (1) a modified Morning Prayer service, ending with a long pastoral prayer; (2) an intermission, consisting of announcements, offering, and hymn; and (3) the sermon, invitation to Christian discipleship, closing hymn, and benediction. The effect was to create two separate half-services in tension with each other. The praise and prayer service was thought of as the "worship" or "liturgy," and the sermon was seen as something separate from worship or liturgy. As one grew, the other shrank. Tensions developed between those who were "liturgical" at the expense of preaching and those who stressed preaching at the expense of worship. More serious yet was the wide separation of the reading of scripture from preaching, with the loss of expectation that preaching would be the interpretation of scripture.

In the years following World War II, many Methodists, convinced that they had lost much of their biblical and historic heritage, made a serious study of John Wesley and rediscovered his great emphasis on scripture and sacrament as "means of grace." They found themselves sharing with other Christians who were rediscovering the common biblical and early Christian roots that underlie our various denominational heritages. One Christian denomination after another undertook to reexamine its worship in the light of the scriptures and the early church and to reform its worship accordingly.

For Methodists this began with a renewed emphasis on scripture. As early as the first edition of *The Book of Worship* (1945) the reading of two scripture lessons was again in the orders of worship. The 1965 edition of *The Book of Worship* and the 1966 edition of *The Methodist Hymnal* continued this pattern and added a lectionary that included three scripture readings (Old Testament, epistle, and gospel), psalter, and a canticle or other act of praise for each Sunday or special day.

For Evangelical United Brethren, whose worship history had been similar to that of the Methodists, the orders of worship in *The Hymnal* (1957) provided two lessons and a responsive reading from the scriptures and suggested that Old Testament, epistle, and gospel be represented in these three readings.

When The United Methodist Church was formed in 1968, and the process began that is described in the Introduction to this book, Wesley's admonition "to follow the scriptures and the primitive church" was taken with great seriousness. This involved both opening up to United Methodists the fruits of the reforms undertaken in other denominations and also making distinctive United Methodist contributions to the ecumenical renewal of worship. Our United Methodist contributions were seen as including both our Methodist and our Evangelical United Brethren heritages, as well as our various ethnic and cultural heritages. The purpose was to give a more adequate shape and content to both the proclamation of the Word and Holy Communion. Our new services, adopted in 1984, are the result.

4. New Theological Understandings

As we United Methodists study and use these Services of Word and Table, some changes from the patterns of our recent past will be evident.

First, there is a clearer emphasis on the centrality of scripture and proclamation. The reading, singing, and hearing of scripture are necessary to the proclamation of the Word in the midst of the congregation. The sermon is part of the proclaiming and hearing of the scriptures, thus emphasizing preaching as a contemporary witness to the Word. The placement of the sermon toward the central part of the service provides for a fuller congregational response to the Word. These services allow for more congregational participation in scripture, read and proclaimed. Indeed, this demonstrates the very root meaning of the word *liturgy:* "the work of the people."

Second, there is a new accent on joyful praise and thanksgiving. This is particularly evident in Holy Communion, where sacrifice (Hebrews 13:15-16) is joined with a clearer note of thanksgiving and celebration of what God has done in Christ. We present ourselves (Romans 12:1) in union with the universal work of Christ and all the gifts God has given us to offer. The very form of the thanksgiving prayers expresses this theological understanding. They are shaped by the Hebrew notion of *berakah:* to bless God and to bless or consecrate something by giving thanks to God for it. Thus, to give thanks is to respond to our creation, to our redemption, and to the promise of God's ultimate victory by offering "our sacrifice of praise and thanksgiving."

Third, a more prominent place is given to *remembrance* as a vivid presentation of the past, which directs us toward our future. *Anamnesis*, which is the New Testament word we translate when we speak of the "remembrance" of Christ in Holy Communion, is not simply the mental act we commonly associate with the word *remember*. It means that we recall (in the sense of "bring back") and reappropriate Christ in the present so that we are caught up into his very being and are continuing the redemptive history of God-with-us. Thus, in our corporate memory, recited and proclaimed, we are given identity in Christ and a foretaste of the ultimate messianic banquet.

Fourth, a more prominent place is given to the Holy Spirit in worship. The living experience of encounter and communion with God in proclamation and praise is accented especially in the prayer for illumination and in the invoking of the Spirit on the people and on the gifts of bread and wine. Holy Communion is marked by an awareness of the Spirit's power and the presence of Jesus Christ in the entire action of Word and Meal. Moreover, the Spirit is seen in the various ministries of the people at prayer and in their work in the world, which is here joined with the work of Christ. Thus a distinctive, though not exclusive, note is sounded in testimony to grace and to experienced life in the Spirit in both Word and Sacrament.

Fifth, the recovery of congregational prayer and praise is at the heart of the people's participation in worship. The variety of prayers in the service, each with its own purposes, points up how richly varied are the types and facets of prayer. The prayers of the people for the church and for the world are an expression of the priesthood of all believers. In these services, a new awareness of prayer as sacramental activity may be brought to life. The people's prayers and praise are indeed "the work of the people of God," thus emphasizing a theology of the laity in worship.

Sixth, Christian worship as expressed in these services is to be celebrated and experienced in the light of the promise of all that God has yet to reveal to us. As God's people we are to love, to serve, and to worship God "between the times" of God's redemptive acts in Christ and the coming in final victory of God in

Christ at the end of history. This idea is emphasized during the Great Thanksgiving in the people's acclamation: "Christ has died, Christ has risen, Christ will come again." Also present is the conviction that our worship through time, including the seasons of the year, can express the richness of this hope and understanding. This joyful foretaste is truly for all seasons.

And so, by holding up the full service of Word and Holy Communion as the norm, these services express a deeper theological understanding of what is meant by *celebration*. In Holy Communion we are given a history more powerful than mere "remembered events" and a future far greater than natural expectation. These are the great gifts of God, who in worship makes us present to one another and God present to us.

5. Practical Problems

There will be problems that need to be faced and questions that need to be discussed if these services are to feel right to persons accustomed to other patterns.

If persons in congregations in which little scripture has been read ask, "Why are we reading so much scripture?" several points can be emphasized. As we have seen, the reading of generous amounts of scripture has been at the heart of classical Christian worship patterns since the earliest Christians adapted for their purposes the scripture centered service of the synagogue. Over time, such worship deeply imprints the whole story and teaching of scripture on the hearts and minds of Christians. If this has *always* been necessary for Christians, it is *especially* so in a day when Christians tend to be both biblically illiterate and immersed in a secular society. Even the minority of Christians who regularly hear and study scripture in church school or at home need the different exposure to scripture that comes when it is read and preached in worship. A great many others will hear no scripture all week other than what they hear in Sunday worship. Finally, we may be confident that the experience of hearing scripture effectively read and preached will enable persons to appreciate for themselves how much they are helped by having the scriptures "opened to them."

In congregations in which the response to the Word has been limited to—at most—invitation to Christian discipleship, hymn, and benediction, careful preparation and interpretation may be necessary to make a fuller response seem right. Suggestions are given in the Commentary of ways in which the response to the Word can be adapted to the needs of various congregations, and further imagination and creativity are encouraged in making a transition from present patterns. The sermon itself may clearly lead into some form of response.

Many persons will ask, "Why does the full order of worship include both the Service of the Word (the preaching service) and the celebration of Holy Communion?" Most United Methodists have been accustomed to only a "preaching service" as the regular pattern for Sunday worship. The Lord's Supper, or Holy Communion, has often been regarded as an occasional service, celebrated quarterly or at best monthly. Many regard Holy Communion as something added on to the "regular" service. *The Book of Worship* (1965) of The Methodist Church and the *Book of Ritual* (1959) of The Evangelical United Brethren Church include full services of Word and Table, but these have not been widely regarded as normal for every Lord's Day.

While we hold Holy Communion following the proclamation of the Word as the scriptural norm for every Lord's Day, it appears that this reform will take longer and be more difficult than the restoration of the full Service of the Word. We have been on a "starvation diet" for a longer time in the case of communion than of scripture, and our appetites have shrunk accordingly. While attendance in some churches goes up on communion Sundays, other churches experience a drop in attendance on days when communion has been announced. Even when attendance is stable or rises on communion Sundays, there still may be resistance to celebrating it more often. Increasing the frequency of communion before a congregation is ready can be counterproductive. It may be more effective to lead a congregation first to experience and understand communion in such a way that they *want* it more often.

One problem concerns the length of the service. In some churches, people are relaxed about the length of their services, but in others there may be serious objection to extending the length of the service beyond an hour. In many churches, the service seems uncomfortably long when Holy Communion is celebrated.

Fortunately, there is no need to lengthen the service beyond what is acceptable to a given congregation. Many congregations, even large membership churches, celebrate both Word and Holy Communion in less than an hour without any sense of being rushed. Where time is a problem, the service may move quickly to the reading and preaching of the Word. The sermon should be at least as strong when communion is celebrated as it is at other times; in fact, preaching may gain strength by being shortened and sharply focused. Most congregations take longer in giving and receiving the bread and cup than is necessary, especially when they have table dismissals. The giving and receiving may be done in a variety of ways, and each congregation can find what is for it the best mode of communing. Specific suggestions are found on pages 67-69 of the commentary that follows.

Another problem is that of maintaining enough variety through the year. One reason for this problem has been the lack of options in our traditional ritual. That ritual, furthermore, tended to reinforce the idea that communion is necessarily solemn and penitential—a tone that is appropriate at some times, but not others. The new services may appropriately be varied from one week or season to another, with an appropriate balance between what varies and what is unchanging. Resources for providing such variety and balance are found in *Holy Communion* (SWR 16, Abingdon Press, 1987) and *Handbook of the Christian Year* (Abingdon Press, 1986).

Another problem is that many persons have experienced communion as uncomfortably "formal"—a complicated sequence of archaic words read from a printed page—or for some other reason culturally strange and unnatural. It need not be so. Holy Communion is a simple and natural sequence of *actions* in which words, while important, are secondary. The words that are used can be as formal or informal, as archaic or as contemporary, as may be appropriate in a given situation. Words, music, and actions can be styled so as to be natural to persons of any ethnic or cultural background.

Still another problem is the need for long-term reeducation in the basic understanding of Holy Communion. Some misunderstandings have become so lodged in people's consciousness that it will require much teaching and experience to dislodge them. Wesley's sermon "The Duty of Constant Communion"[10] is helpful to read as an example of the teaching that is needed.

Those who fear that if they receive communion more often it will mean less can discover that the opposite is the case. This fear is often expressed in churches where communion has been an occasional service of rededication held only at times like New Year's, Holy Week, or World Communion Sunday. Occasional reaffirmation of God's covenant with us is indeed important, and this is effectively provided for in the new Baptismal Covenant services. While communion on such occasions is surely appropriate, we deprive ourselves if we limit it to those times and limit its wealth of meanings to simply rededication. Good preaching and teaching over a period of time on the many meanings of communion will help, and even more helpful will be the power of experience. "Appetites" shrunken from chronic underfeeding will grow as people feed at the Lord's table.

Those who believe that the renewed emphasis on communion is "too Catholic" can learn that it is at the heart of the Protestant heritage given us by Luther, Calvin, and Wesley. One of the things these reformers were protesting against in sixteenth-century Roman Catholicism (and the eighteenth century Church of England) was infrequent communion by the people. It was the ingrained habit of infrequent communion that the people had carried over from medieval catholicism that led them to resist the Reformation call for the Lord's Supper every Lord's Day. Indeed, the Roman Catholic Church suffered from infrequent communion by its people from the Middle Ages until its reforms in our own century.

Those who feel "unworthy" to receive communion can, through teaching and pastoral care, come to receive it as God's free gift and means of grace. They may have misunderstood Paul's warning:

> Whoever, therefore, eats the bread or drinks the cup of the Lord in an unworthy manner will be guilty of profaning the body and blood of the Lord. . . . For any one who eats and drinks without discerning the body eats and drinks judgment upon himself. (I Corinthians 11:27, 29)

If we read the whole passage (verses 17-34), we discover that Paul was referring to a situation in the church at Corinth, where persons were bringing their own food and drink and sometimes eating and drinking to excess while refusing to share with those who had brought nothing and were going hungry. These persons were obviously communing in an unworthy manner. They failed to discern the body of Christ—the hungry people right there in front of them who were members of Christ's body. Receiving communion in a worthy manner is not at all the same as receiving it because we think we are worthy. The only way any of us is worthy is through God's free gift in the Christ who liked to eat with sinners (Luke 15:2)—and still does.

Those who have had a one-sided understanding or experience of Holy Communion can grow to a greater appreciation of the many-sided richness of meanings in this sacrament. If it has been for them sad and funereal, it can become for them joyous and triumphant. If it has been for them a celebration of all God's mighty acts in Jesus Christ and suitable for Christmas and Easter and every Lord's Day. If it has been for them simply a reminder of Christ's death and, therefore, suited only to somber times, such as Holy Week, it can become for them a celebration of all God's mighty acts in Jesus Christ and suitable for Christmas and Easter and every Lord's Day. If it has been for them simply a memorial of what Christ has already done, it can become a resurrection meal with the living Christ and a foretaste of the heavenly banquet. If Holy Communion has seemed incredible or offensive to them because of some interpretation they were taught, they can learn other interpretations. Congregational study of James F. White's *Sacraments as God's Self-Giving* (Abingdon, 1983) or William H. Willimon's *Sunday Dinner* (The Upper Room, 1981) can be helpful. Members of a church may hold differing interpretations of Holy Communion, and these interpretations may all be affirmed as facets of a mystery that none of us can fully grasp.

Ultimately, the communion we have with God in Jesus Christ is a mystery. "This mystery, which is Christ in you, the hope of glory" (Colossians 1:27) is "the mystery of the gospel" (Ephesians 6:19). None of us is so wise as to have plumbed the depths of this mystery.

Yet, the mystery of the gospel is revealed even to young children—perhaps *especially* to young children, if we remember

Jesus' words (Mark 10:13-16). Children can join youth and adults in receiving communion, as all are one in Christ.

Holy Communion is a means of grace that works through all the senses, on many different levels, and in ways that are appropriate to persons of every age and stage of development. A small child who is present at this holy meal knows the difference between being accepted and rejected at a meal table, connects being fed with being loved, and is receiving the grace of the One who loves to take children in his arms and bless them. On the other hand, the wisest saint can sing with Charles Wesley:

> Sure and real is the grace,
> The manner be unknown;
> Only meet us in thy ways
> And perfect us in one.
> Let us taste the heavenly powers;
> Lord, we ask for nothing more.
> Thine to bless, 'tis only ours
> To wonder and adore.[11]

6. An Extraordinary Opportunity

In recent years, there has been a widespread recovery among United Methodists of the Service of the Word. With the greatly increased use of the lectionary, much more scripture is being read in public worship. Preaching is increasingly based on part or all of the scriptures that have been read in the service. Increasingly, congregations are praying and praising through the psalter. Not only are churches singing psalmody, but other hymn and anthem texts as well are often words or paraphrases of scripture.

There has also been a growing movement among United Methodists to increase the frequency with which the full service of Word and Table is celebrated. A small, but growing, minority of United Methodists celebrate and receive communion weekly.

With these new services, we now have an extraordinary opportunity to recover what John Wesley advocated and practiced: "constant communion." With these resources, we can also move toward life as the people of God in a new ecumenical spirit, seeking to be truly evangelical, reformed, and catholic, while yet treasuring our distinctive United Methodist emphases. The whole of our faith is focused on the proclaiming of the good news in Christ, the sharing at the Lord's table with those who have been incorporated into Christ's death and resurrection through Christian baptism, and the living out of that life in Christian service. Thus, renewal of our worship is deeply interwoven with renewal of church discipline and with the spiritual renewal of the life of Christ in our midst.

We express the hope that the full service of Word and Sacrament will eventually become normative for United Methodist worship on the Lord's Day. In the meantime, whether or not the service on a given Sunday includes Holy Communion, we can at least recover the basic shape and intent of the full order of Word and Table. The basic pattern of worship can be a vehicle for enabling the congregation to experience Christ more fully in the worshiping assembly. The presence of Christ is known, by the aid of the Holy Spirit, in the congregation gathered in Christ's name, in scripture and proclamation, and in prayer and praise, even when the full experience of the Word is not completed in the celebration of the Meal. By this, we can recognize that Christ is present to his people in many ways. We can deepen our understanding of the relationship of gathering, proclaiming, and responding, to the mystery of our communion with the living Christ and with one another as members of his body. In this way, we have the promise of the unfathomable riches of Christ at the heart of our common worship.

B. Commentary on the Order

1. The Entrance

The first major part of the service is known as "the entrance rite," or simply "the entrance." The people are not simply entering the place of worship; they are also entering into an encounter with the living God, through the risen Christ, in the power of the Holy Spirit. Some have used the terms *approach* or *preparation* in describing this part of the service. The people come together in the Lord's name; there may then be greetings, music and song, prayer and praise. This part of our worship should be uncluttered and serve to bring us to full, conscious participation. It should neither be unduly dramatic nor a prolonged series of devotional exercises. This is a classic pattern of entrance, but what is most important is that the congregation enter into readiness for the reading, preaching, and hearing of the Word, which is to follow.

a. Gathering

The worship service begins when the people gather for worship. While they are gathering, what they are doing expresses that they are coming together in the Lord's name. This time is both an "outward and visible" gathering of the people and also an "inward and spiritual" gathering—a putting aside of inner preoccupations, a "getting it all together," a focusing of awareness that they are a people gathered in the presence of the Lord.

Several different patterns are found in United Methodist congregations. (1) informal greetings, conversation, and fellowship; (2) announcements and welcoming; (3) rehearsal of congregational music and other acts of worship that are unfamiliar to the people; (4) informal prayer, singing, and/or testimony; (5) quiet meditation and private prayer; and (6) organ or other instrumental or vocal music. These may be combined in some appropriate order: (1) may be encouraged before the music begins or before persons have entered the place of worship; (5) and (6) may take place together following (2), (3), or (4). Sometimes it is possible to relate the music to the theme or the music of the service as a whole, and this can be especially effective in focusing the people's attention.

None of these patterns in itself is more valid than another, but one pattern may be far more appropriate than another, depending on the congregation, the specific circumstances of the day, and the nature of the service itself. Some congregations find it best to vary their pattern of gathering; others find one pattern that is best for them all the time.

b. Greeting and Hymn

Facing the people, the leader greets them in the Lord's name. This is no mere secular greeting, such as exchanging "Good morning." Scripture sentences or responsive acts between the leader and people declare that the Lord is present and empowers our worship. A simple greeting, used over a period of time and easily memorized, can be both natural and effectively serve this purpose.

The hymn may precede or follow the greeting. It is appropriate that the people, having been greeted in the Lord's name, return the greeting to God with a hymn of praise. On the other hand, where the architecture of the worship space or the nature of the occasion calls for an entrance of choir and worship leaders, this processional hymn or entrance song should come *before* the greeting, allowing the greeting to be spoken facing the people rather than from behind them.

The opening hymn is most appropriately corporate praise to God, theologically related to the principal attributes of God that call forth gratitude and praise. The music and the text should both be strong.

An entrance song may be restrained and formal, or it may be festive and spontaneous, depending on the context. It is the joyous movement of musicians and leaders toward the focus of gathered attentiveness to God. Processions may include a cross, candles, Bible, and banners.

Where the size of the congregation and the design of the building permit, a congregation may wish on certain occasions to have the entire community move into place during an entrance song, perhaps following preparatory prayers or other activities elsewhere.

In any event, it is appropriate to stand during the singing of this hymn. Printed or verbal invitations to stand, here or elsewhere in the service, should show sensitivity to the fact that some persons cannot stand. Use of phrases such as "are invited to stand" or "may stand," or the simple gesture of upturned palms, are more inclusive than words that sound like a command to stand or an assumption that everyone will stand.

c. Opening Prayer(s) and Praise

Prayer at the opening of worship, together with singing addressed to God, establishes that our worship is a communion with the living God as well as with one another. It includes recognition of who we are before God by centering upon the nature and gifts of God.

A great variety of types and forms of opening prayer is possible, provided that we know what the point of our prayer-action is and how it works with other parts of the service. An opening prayer should intensify the congregation's awareness of its activity, while moving toward the acts of worship that follow. Three major patterns are suggested.

1. There may be a *prayer of the day*, which may be a collect. It may either be a prayer suited for any occasion, or any Lord's day, or it may address God in the light of the theme of the day. It may be prayed in unison or led by one person. It may be preceded or followed by silence. It may be extemporaneous, but it should be brief and to the point.

2. There may be a *prayer of confession and act of pardon*. This may include a sequence of (a) call to confession, (b) prayer of confession, (c) silence, and (d) declaration of pardon. A prayer of confession and declaration of pardon belong together; neither should be used without the other. The four examples on pages 42-43 of *The Book of Services* illustrate the variety of ways in which the declaration of pardon may be made.

3. There may be a *litany*, such as the "Lord, have mercy" on pages 35-36 of *The Book of Services*. This litany is an ancient treasure that can either be sung or spoken.

This service is flexible with regard to the placement of confession and pardon. United Methodists have two traditions in this regard. Prior to 1964, the confession and pardon were always after the proclamation of the Word when Holy Communion was celebrated, and this remained the pattern in the 1964 brief form of Holy Communion. On the other hand, the order of Sunday worship without communion, which had not mentioned confession and pardon before 1932, began at that time to make provision for them near the opening of worship, following the pattern of Anglican Morning Prayer. This pattern was continued and extended to the complete form of Holy Communion in 1964. While the printed texts of the new services place confession and pardon after the proclamation of the Word, the basic order indicates that they may be placed at either of the traditional points in the service.

There is no single correct posture for the congregation during prayer. The biblical tradition of standing to pray is always appropriate, especially when the people have been standing for praise immediately before, and perhaps after, the prayer. Kneeling for prayer is also appropriate, especially in confession. Praying seated and bowed is acceptable, especially if the alternatives are for persons to be kept standing or kneeling for an uncomfortable length of time.

If an act of praise is desired after the opening prayer(s), one or more of the following may be spoken or sung: (1) The "Glory to God in the Highest," (2) a psalm or other scripture song, (3) The *Gloria Patri*, or (4) an anthem.

This is one point in the service where choirs commonly sing, though they may also sing between the lessons or at the time of the offering. The character of the music, however, should suggest its appropriate placement in the order of worship. A musical text praising God for pardoning mercy, for instance, would be most fitting following confession and pardon. A musical text that is a prayer for others best occurs along with the spoken intercessions. A general anthem of praise is usually appropriate at various points in the service. Since it is best, when possible, to include the whole congregation in acts of praise, there is a growing movement toward the use of musical forms in which the whole congregation has a familiar or easily learned part to sing.

Ancient and biblical acts of praise are the most traditional at this point in the service, and there is much to be said for their use. These are more effective if sung—by the whole congregation, if possible. Some, such as the *Gloria Patri*, certainly may be sung by any congregation. On the other hand, many settings of such texts as the "Glory to God in the Highest" (*Gloria in Excelsis*) are too difficult for most congregations to sing and are better suited to choirs.

Other possibilities for an act of praise at this point include a hymn, hymn stanza, chorus, doxology, or a spoken litany of praise.

2. Proclamation and Response

The second and central part of the service is called Proclamation and Response. It is the service of the Word. From the earliest times, the scriptures, read and proclaimed, have constituted the heart of the teaching and preaching of the church. This pattern of worship is designed to reassert the primacy of scripture and the direct relation of the scripture to preaching and response. United Methodist worship has often failed to provide adequate coverage of the Bible. Often there has been little attention given to the systematic presentation of the Bible over a period of time.

This whole section of the service should be regarded as one coherent movement. Those who participated in the testing of this service in its earlier stages will remember that what is now a single section called "Proclamation and Response" was at first given as two sections: "Proclamation and Praise" followed by "Responses and Offerings." Testing in our own denomination, ecumenical consultations, and further reflection revealed that such a division broke up what should be experienced as a unity and failed to do justice to the call-and-response pattern that structures the Proclamation and Response as a whole.

This call-and-response pattern acts out the constant reality of God's call and our response. To be sure, we often experience God's response to our call, but at a deeper level we would not be able to call to God were it not in response to God's prior call to us. This rhythm of call and response occurs simultaneously on many "frequencies." Our earlier insight that the whole time from the first reading of scripture through the sermon is primarily proclamation (call) and that the whole time after the sermon through the offering is primarily response is correct as far as it goes. On the other hand, the scripture readings are interspersed with responses of praise, and there is a proclamation-and-response pattern in the later sequence of Invitation-Confession-Pardon-Peace-Offering. Then, too, within any given act of worship there is a constant interplay of proclamation (call) and response as worshipers are responding in their hearts and even outwardly in words or body language to proclamation, and as congregational singing and other responses function also as proclamation.

a. Prayer for Illumination

This prayer serves as a bridge between the initial section of the service (entrance) and the proclamation of the Word.

This prayer asks for the Holy Spirit's guidance and power on the reader and preacher in proclaiming the Word of God and on the people in their hearing, understanding, and responding. In many churches, this prayer is either prayed in unison by the congregation or led by a layperson. If the preceding act of praise has been omitted, prayer for illumination can be included in the opening prayers. In some instances, the prayer for the day or collect will serve as a prayer for illumination.

b. Scripture

The historic practice of following a lectionary, or regular cycle of scripture lessons, has much to commend it. The three-year Common Lectionary (see chapter 2 below) includes for each Sunday a first reading (usually from the Old Testament), a second reading (usually from some part of the New Testament other than the Gospels), and a reading from one of the four Gospels.

When scripture is read, the visual impact, as well as the sound, is important. Reading the lessons from a large pulpit Bible that all the people can see shows forcefully the importance of scripture in worship. In some congregations, the Bible is brought in as part of the opening procession, placed on the pulpit, and opened at the beginning of the proclamation of the Word. When this Bible remains open in front of the preacher during the sermon, it emphasizes visually that the sermon comes from the scriptures.

In many congregations, one or more of the scripture lessons are read by a layperson. This follows ancient custom and is one of the ways laypersons can effectively share in the leadership of worship. By their careful preparation of the reading and by their sense of the importance of their ministry, readers of scripture can make the reading of scripture one among the high points of the service. It is both fair to all segments of the congregation and also more interesting and effective if the readers chosen over a period of time represent, in fair proportions, women and men, youth and young adults as well as middle and older adults, and whatever ethnic and cultural variety is in the congregation. The lay reader often sits in the congregation until time for the reading and then comes forward. This is a way of involving the congregation more closely in the reading and of not separating the reader from family or from the rest of the people.

Special thought should be given to the words used to introduce and close the reading of scripture. Introductory comments, explaining the setting of the scripture readings, are often appropriate, but they should be brief and to the point. Readings may be immediately preceded by such words as: "Hear the Word of God in a reading from _____." In closing, the reader may say, "This is the Word of the Lord," to which the people may respond, "Thanks be to God." Or the reader may say simply, "Amen," to which the people may respond, "Amen."

Scripture can be presented in other ways. The congregation may follow the reading silently in their own Bibles or in pew Bibles, read in unison, or join with the reader in some responsive or antiphonal pattern. Stories or parables may be dramatized or danced. There may be visual or instrumental accompaniment.

The scripture readings may be interspersed with (1) a psalm or psalm portions, sung or spoken, after the first reading and (2) a hymn or song related to the scriptures of the day, or a sung alleluia, before the final reading. The rhythm of proclamation and response in this part of the service is a prime example of the call-and-response pattern that is so fundamental to our worship in general. God's Word comes to us through scripture, and we respond with praise.

The use of an appropriate psalm or psalm portions as an act of praise is derived from ancient Jewish and Christian practice. When a psalm is used as an act of praise, it is appropriate for the congregation to stand and for the psalm to be followed by the saying or singing of the "Glory to the Father" (*Gloria Patri*). In this use, the psalms are not properly Old Testament lessons and should not be considered substitutes for the reading from the Old Testament. There is a variety of ways in which psalms may be spoken or sung as praise, and we are in an exciting time during which the psalms are being rediscovered as prayer and praise. The psalms are even more effective when sung than when spoken, and churches are urged to investigate new and old ways in which psalms may be sung by congregation, choir, and soloist (cantor).

Traditionally an alleluia has been sung before the reading of the Gospel, and this remains an effective practice today. Alternatively, a "hymn of preparation" (for the Gospel and sermon) may be sung. In either case, it is traditional for the congregation to be invited to stand for the singing and remain standing for the gospel. In the gospel, we are addressed by the words of Christ and in a very special way experience this as an encounter with the risen, living Christ. To stand and greet Christ with an alleluia and remain standing while Christ speaks to us is an act of respect that has seemed natural to a great many Christians. It is not meant to imply that God's Word is less present in other portions of the Bible, nor should it be forced on congregations where it is not perceived as appropriate.

The full and ancient pattern of three readings, interspersed with psalter and singing, is recommended; but where constraint of time or other pastoral considerations dictate, this can be shortened to two readings, interspersed with a single act of praise, without detracting from the integrity of the service. If only two readings are used regularly, care should be taken to present the whole biblical message over a period of time.

c. Sermon

The placement of the sermon at this central point in the service is in keeping both with its central importance and with its linkage to scripture. The reading and preaching of the Bible are so closely related that nothing ought to come between them. To emphasize this unity, the ancient and ecumenical practice of placing the sermon immediately following the last reading is strongly recommended. Some ministers pray immediately before preaching, but if one takes seriously the unity of reading and preaching in the proclamation of the Word, it would seem more fitting to invoke God's help in the prayer for illumination at the beginning of the whole proclamation and response section of the service, as suggested above.

When two or three scripture lessons have been read, it is not necessary to preach on both or all of them; it is enough to preach on one of them. In some traditions, it is customary always to preach from the Gospel, but in others, such as ours, it is also considered appropriate to preach from one of the earlier lessons or from the psalm. Those who preach from the Common

Lectionary will find that from Christ the King Sunday through the Baptism of the Lord and from Transfiguration Sunday through Easter Day the three readings usually are linked, thematically or in some other fashion; it may be quite possible to relate them all to the sermon. During the rest of the year, except for an occasional festival or special day, this is not the case, and it is left to the preacher to choose which scripture to preach from. During the half-year after Pentecost, each of the three readings goes from Sunday to Sunday in its own semi-continuous cycle, so that it is left to the preacher to choose whether to preach from the Old Testament cycle, the epistle cycle, or the Gospel cycle. Thus during that half of the year it is possible to find in the lectionary a nine-year preaching cycle.

Preaching is fully as important on communion Sundays as on other occasions. The omission of preaching on communion Sundays violates the unity of Word and Sacrament. This does not mean that it is necessary to preach on the subject of Holy Communion every time it is celebrated; any facet of the gospel can be preached in such a way that it leads appropriately to the celebration of Holy Communion. On the other hand, in congregations where misunderstanding of the sacrament is causing persons to stay away on communion Sundays, it may be well to preach about Holy Communion when it is *not* being celebrated, so that all hear a more adequate biblical and theological understanding of its meaning.

The sermon is often strengthened by being conceived in flexible and imaginative terms. A short sermon may be fully as effective as a long one and should not be called a sermonette or a meditation. Dialogue, dramatization, audiovisual accompaniment, use of objects, and active congregational participation are among the many possibilities for preaching. Lay speaking or lay witnessing, drama (live or on film or videotape), or a musical presentation that proclaims the Word can on occasion constitute the sermon.

d. Response to the Word

Preaching calls for a response. In the rhythm of proclamation and response, the gospel/sermon is a long and climactic proclamation (call), which is appropriately answered by a long and climactic response. The ultimate response to God's Word is found in our daily faith and life, but an immediate response is also important. If we are to go out as Christians into our daily world, we need the strength and focus that comes from affirming our *commitment* to what has been proclaimed—our *ownership* of what we have heard. This vital part of the service is neglected in many congregations, and one of the advantages of the new service is in the way the response to the Word has been strengthened.

The phrase "response to the Word," though it will be new to many, has a rich variety of meaning and possibilities. It is to be understood here as indicating a specific occasion for decision, witness, or reflection in accord with the content of the proclamation. Immediately following the sermon, any one or more of the following actions are appropriate.

1. An invitation to Christian discipleship, followed by a hymn of invitation or of response, or a baptism or confirmation hymn. This invitation for commitment to Christ and his church may lead into any of the other responses to the Word listed below or to specific courses of action or into the concerns and prayers of the church.

2. Baptism, confirmation, profession or reaffirmation of faith, reception into membership from another denomination or from another United Methodist congregation, recognitions, dedications, or other special congregational acts. See chapter 3 below.

3. A creed or affirmation of faith. When a service of the baptismal covenant is used (see chapter 3), it is appropriate that all those present be invited to reaffirm their faith at the time the Apostles' Creed is used. On Sundays when this rite is not used, use of the Apostles' Creed, the Nicene Creed, or a modern affirmation at the same point in the service where a baptism would take place serves to remind us of our baptism and of the faith in which we were baptized.

4. Silent reflection and spoken expressions from the congregation. These may take various forms. There may be a period of corporate silence, broken as persons are moved to witness, pray, or sing. There may be response to the sermon

on the part of one or more "reactors" or an open "talk-back" session. Local traditions and the character of the proclamation that has just taken place will determine what is appropriate.

e. Concerns and Prayers

This has been known by some United Methodists as the pastoral prayer, but the phrase "concerns and prayers" better indicates that the whole church family is at prayer.

Before the time of prayer itself, persons in the congregation may express joys and concerns that they would like included in the prayers. If the congregation is too large for persons to be heard when they speak out, prayer requests may be written on cards and either deposited in an appropriately marked box or brought forward by ushers. Persons may also express their prayer requests personally to the leader during the week before the service. In some situations the concerns expressed may call for a specific commitment to an act of service.

The time of prayer itself should include any joys and concerns that have been expressed and may take one or more of these forms:

1. Brief *intercessions, petitions, and thanksgivings* may be prayed by the leader. If there has been no prior opportunity for prayer requests, members of the congregation may be invited to pray brief spontaneous intercessions, petitions, or thanksgivings. In either case, each brief prayer may be followed by a common response—such as, "Lord, hear our prayer"—spoken or sung by all.

2. A *litany or unison prayer* of intercession and petition may be prayed. Examples are found on pages 39-41 of *The Book of Services.*

3. A *pastoral prayer* may be offered.

At this, or some other, time during the service, persons so desiring may be invited to kneel for prayer at the communion rail. Such an invitation is often called "the altar call," although others apply this term to the invitation to Christian discipleship.

The size and character of the congregation and of the space in which they worship will help to indicate which of these forms is most practicable and effective.

It is crucial that these be the prayers of the congregation, whether expressed directly by the people or indirectly through the leader, and that they be seen and experienced as such by the people. This is a time for prayers that are as specific as possible—intercessions for persons or causes, petitions for particular needs, and thanksgivings for recent blessings. These concerns and prayers are responses to the Word and part of the people's offerings. These acts connect prayer and Christian action in the world.

f. Confession, Pardon, and Peace

When there has not been an act of confession and pardon earlier in the service, the minister leads the congregation in the following sequence:

1. Call to confession. Since the sequence of call, confession, pardon, peace, and offering serves as a bridge between the service of the Word and the service of the table, this call also serves as an invitation to the Lord's table when Holy Communion is being celebrated. For this reason, it is sometimes referred to as the invitation. Set texts may be used—such as those on pages 21, 27, and 31 of *The Book of Services*—or the call may be informal.
2. Prayer of confession. Examples are found on pages 41-42 of *The Book of Services*. Confession can also take the form of a litany, with a response such as "Lord, have mercy," or "Forgive us, O God." It is sometimes very effective to sing the prayer of confession. Hymns such as "Spirit of God, Descend upon My Heart" (stanzas 1, 2, 5) and "Dear Master, in Whose Life I See" may be sung as prayers of confession.
3. All pray in silence.
4. Declaration of pardon. The minister declares God's pardon for those penitent, using forms such as those on pages 42-43 of *The Book of Services*. This act should always follow a prayer of confession. It may take the form of a mutual declaration between minister and people, a declaration by the minister, scriptural words of assurance, or a prayer for pardon led by the minister.

5. The peace. The people may offer one another signs of reconciliation and love, particularly when Holy Communion is celebrated. Both the traditional and the new invitations to confession and communion call those who repent of their sin and who also seek to live in peace (love and charity) with one another. Having made or renewed peace with God through confession and pardon, it is fitting that we now make or renew peace with one another. When the peace is immediately followed by the offering, we recall the words of Matthew 5:23-24: "If you are offering your gift at the altar, and there remember that your brother [or sister] has something against you, leave your gift there before the altar and go; first be reconciled to your brother [or sister], and then come and offer your gift." The New Testament Christian practice of exchanging the peace ("a holy kiss," "the kiss of love") is mentioned in Romans 16:16, I Corinthians 16:20, II Corinthians 13:12, I Thessalonians 5:26, and I Peter 5:14. Since peace is the gift of God's grace through Jesus Christ, it is not simply *our* peace but the peace of *Christ* that we are offering one another.

Because the peace is new to many people, and can be an uncomfortable experience for some, it needs special interpretation. It is not simply greetings all around; it is an act of blessing. The gestures and words used may vary widely, depending on the character of the congregation and the nature of the occasion. For some, it will be a gesture primarily of love, for others primarily of reconciliation. Depending on the seating arrangement and the degree of intimacy perceived as authentic for the people, this act may consist in a simple handshake, a clasping of both hands, an embrace, or a kiss. The words used may be elaborate ("The peace of the Lord be with you." "And also with you.") or simple ("Peace." "Amen."). They may also be spontaneous, as individuals are moved. Intensity and significance may vary from time to time, and genuine differences of temperament and conviction should be respected.

g. Offering

The offering is more than money; it is the symbolic offering to God of ourselves and all that we have. It is the corporate self-giving of God's people, in the spirit of Romans 12:1, "Offer yourselves as a living sacrifice to God, dedicated to his service and pleasing to him" (GNB). This is the mystery of giving back to God the gifts of God's creation, including signs of our labor, so that we know that all we have and are is a trust from God. In addition to money, other appropriate gifts may be offered, such as memorial gifts or other items to be dedicated. If Holy Communion is to follow, the bread and wine are brought by representatives of the people to the Lord's table with the other gifts, or uncovered if already in place. While the offering is being received, there may be instrumental or choral music or congregational singing. When the offering is brought forward and laid on the Lord's table, it is fitting that the congregation stand and that a doxology or other appropriate stanza be sung.

3. Thanksgiving and Communion

What follows the offering depends on whether or not Holy Communion is to be celebrated, but in either event the character of the next part of the service is that of thanksgiving. The offering, with or without the preceding confession-pardon-peace sequence, forms a bridge into this thanksgiving. This is a thanksgiving for all God's mighty acts in Jesus Christ—the whole good news that is the gospel. We shall first consider this thanksgiving on occasions when Holy Communion is not celebrated and then consider the supreme thanksgiving that is Holy Communion.

a. When Holy Communion Is Not Celebrated

On occasions when Holy Communion is *not* celebrated, the service may still incorporate the elements of thanksgiving and sharing that are more fully expressed in Holy Communion.

A prayer of thanksgiving follows the offering, in the place of the Great Thanksgiving. While it has been common to follow the presentation of the offering with a prayer, such a prayer has often had too narrow a focus. This prayer should focus not on the money but on the reality and mighty acts of God in Jesus Christ. It is not a blessing of the money, but a blessing of God. In this sense, it should reflect the Great Thanksgiving over the bread and cup and should anticipate the next celebration of Holy Communion.

Opinion differs as to whether parts of the Great Thanksgiving text itself should be used in a prayer of thanksgiving when Holy Communion is not being celebrated. Pages 22-25 of some editions of *The Book of Services* show how this can be done, omitting the sections marked by a vertical line, which pertain only to Holy Communion. This every-Sunday use of parts of the Great Thanksgiving text permits the congregation to become thoroughly familiar with the opening dialogue and with their cues and responses during this prayer. Thus they may feel more at home with the liturgy when Holy Communion is celebrated, especially if they sing the responses. On the other hand, use of an entirely different prayer of thanksgiving is favored by many who want clearly to differentiate the Great Thanksgiving from all other prayers of thanksgiving. The pattern of giving thanks for God's mighty acts in Jesus Christ and then offering ourselves to God in praise and thanksgiving can be followed, using words that are not associated with Holy Communion. The prayer of thanksgiving on page 181 of *The Book of Worship* (1965) provides a classic model for such a prayer.

The Lord's Prayer is a fitting act of unison prayer at the conclusion of this thanksgiving, as at the conclusion of the Great Thanksgiving.

A time of silence may follow the Lord's Prayer, where breaking the bread and giving the bread and cup would be if Holy Communion were being celebrated. This can be a silent sharing (*koinonia*, communion) with God, which suggests and echoes the sharing with God in Holy Communion.

The service then concludes with the Sending Forth (final hymn, dismissal, and going forth).

b. Taking the Bread and Cup

If Holy Communion *is* to be celebrated, the minister then takes the bread and cup, which have been brought forward or uncovered, and does any necessary preparation of the bread and wine.

The bread and wine may be presented in various ways. (1) They may be brought forward with, or immediately following, the money offering by those who have prepared them or by other persons from the congregation. (2) All the people may come forward past the Lord's table to present their offerings, and the presentation of the communion elements may be included in this action. (3) The elements may already be on the table and covered during the first part of the service and may be uncovered during or immediately following the offering.

After taking or uncovering the elements, the minister does any necessary preparation of the bread and wine. The bread should not be broken at this time, but if the wine is in a flagon or cruet, some of it may be poured into the cup. This whole action is nonverbal. It may be done in complete silence. No prayer is necessary before the offering or as the money and the bread and wine are being presented, since the Great Thanksgiving that is to follow includes everything that needs to be said.

The fact that Holy Communion has since early Christian times usually been a token meal of bread and wine, rather than a complete meal, need not trouble us. In our everyday lives we often take part in token meals that fulfill the communal or bonding purposes of eating and drinking together on occasions when we do not need or want a complete meal. When we visit a friend or attend a party or take a break at work, we consider token eating and drinking perfectly natural even if it isn't mealtime and we aren't especially hungry.

Nevertheless, it is important to remember that Holy Communion is a meal, and increasingly churches are celebrating it in ways that make its character as a meal more evident. Real bread is used instead of wafers or pellets that neither look nor taste like bread. Using a large uncut loaf, which later in the service can be broken in full view of the congregation and then distributed to the people, follows the New Testament practice reported in I Corinthians 10:16-17 and is symbolically much more powerful than pre-cutting bread into little cubes. The symbol of a large cup, commonly called the "chalice," on the Lord's table is also powerful, even if the people are to be drinking from individual cups. For Holy Communion, the use of food and drink that looks, feels, tastes, and smells like real food and drink can deepen our awareness of the relationships between God's gifts of creation and redemption. Because Holy Communion is a meal, it is basically a series of actions and is more and more being understood and celebrated as such.

Taking the bread and cup is the first of the four basic actions of Holy Communion. These are based on the New Testament accounts that tell us what Jesus did at the supper on the night before his death. He took bread, gave thanks, broke the bread, and gave it to his disciples. After supper he took the cup, gave thanks, and gave it to his disciples. Therefore, (1) as Jesus took the bread and the cup, so do we; (2) as Jesus gave thanks over the bread and cup, so do we; (3) as Jesus broke the bread, so do we; and (4) as Jesus gave the bread and cup to his disciples, so we give them to one another. Since the first and third of these actions are very brief and preliminary to the second and fourth, we might see these steps as two: (1) taking the bread and cup and giving thanks over them, and (2) breaking the bread and giving the bread and cup to one another. These two steps may be referred to simply as thanksgiving and communion.

It is evident that Holy Communion is far more than words. Indeed, in our celebrations the verbal is often overdone and the four basic actions neglected. Only the second of these actions is primarily verbal; the other three are primarily nonverbal.

It is significant that no one name for the service of Word and table, or for the service of the table, has been universally adopted by Christians. Several names come from the New Testament, and each of them points up certain of the many meanings to be found. (1) The title "The Lord's Supper," found in I Corinthians 11:20, points up the fact that it is a meal and that Christ the Lord is the Host who invites us to this meal. (2) The term "Eucharist" is the English form of the New Testament Greek word *eucharistia,* which means "thanksgiving." It reminds us that Jesus gave thanks to God before sharing the bread and the cup, and it points up the dimension of thanksgiving, which pervades the service of the table. The Great Thanksgiving is sometimes called "the Eucharistic Prayer." The terms *Eucharist* and *Eucharistic Liturgy* are used more broadly to refer to the service of the table or even to the whole service of Word and table. (3) The phrase "the Breaking of Bread," found in Acts 2:42, not only refers specifically to the third of our four actions at the Lord's table, but is also sometimes used to refer to the whole service of the table. (4) The term *communion* is the King James translation of the New Testament Greek word *koinonia* in I Corinthians 10:16, which is translated "participation" in the Revised Standard Version and "sharing" in the Good News and New English Bibles. It points up the fourth of our four actions at the Lord's table and in is narrower sense refers specifically to the giving (sharing) of the bread and cup. In its broader sense, referring to the whole service of the table, it is often called "Holy Communion." This is the name used in *The Book of Services* for the service of the table. This variety of terms reminds us that what happens at the Lord's table is a mystery that goes beyond the power of any one term to describe.

c. The Great Thanksgiving

The Great Thanksgiving includes what had formerly been considered several separate prayers, chiefly the prayer of consecration. There was one great prayer of thanksgiving in the early church, but in the Middle Ages this simplicity and unity were lost and are only now being recovered in our tradition and in the ecumenical church.

This great prayer is a Christian version of the type of Jewish table blessing which Jesus undoubtedly used. In the New Testament, what was done is described both with the verb *bless* (*eulogeo*, as in Matthew 14:19, 26:26; Mark 6:41, 8:7, 14:22; Luke 24:30; and I Corinthians 10:16) and with the verb *give thanks* (*eucharisteo*, as in Matthew 15:36, 26:27; Mark 8:6, 14:23; Luke 22:17 and 19; John 6:11 and 23; and I Corinthians 11:24). In ancient Hebrew tradition, the food and drink are blessed by blessing the name of God and recalling God's mighty acts.

The Great Thanksgiving likewise recalls God's mighty acts from a Christian perspective. It blesses God for God's gifts of creation and redemption, tells the meaning of our actions at the Lord's table, and invokes the power of the Holy Spirit. It is the very heartbeat of what we proclaim and live as a community of the creation, crucifixion, and resurrection, who know the presence of the living Christ and look for his final victory.

This prayer is led by a minister authorized to administer Holy Communion, but congregational participation is also provided for. The ancient Christian practice was for the presiding minister to stand behind the Lord's table facing the people, so that minister and people together are gathered around the table; increasingly this practice is being restored. If the people are not already standing for the presentation of the offering, they should be invited to stand before the opening dialogue of the Great Thanksgiving. The responses should be sung or said by the entire congregation.

Where circumstances permit, especially in smaller congregations, the whole congregation may come forward from where they have been seated and stand around the Lord's table for the whole service of the table. The taking of the bread and cup is an appropriate time for this coming forward to take place, but it might also take place earlier at the invitation to confession or later as the people come to receive communion.

The Book of Services provides four versions of the Great Thanksgiving: (1) The complete text (pages 23-25) is the basis for the other texts. (2) The brief text (pages 28-29) contains the essential portions of the complete text, with four periods (. . . .) marking points at which the presiding minister has the option of inserting either the missing portions of the complete text or other words appropriate to the day or season. (3) The minimum text (pages 31-32) is intended for use with the sick and shut-in and in other situations where brevity is essential and where the ability of persons to make verbal responses may, in varying degrees, be limited. (4) "An Order of Sunday Worship" (pages 16-17) provides an order for the Great Thanksgiving that gives the people's responses with cue lines, while providing the presiding minister freedom to choose or to create an appropriate text. In some situations, the Great Thanksgiving may be prayed more effectively in a print oriented fashion with the whole text in front of the people, while in other situations it may be prayed more effectively in an oral fashion with the people having only cue lines and responses that can readily be memorized. *The Book of Services* provides for both options.

A variety of alternate texts for the Great Thanksgiving and for the rest of the service of the table is found in the book *Holy Communion,* published as Supplemental Worship Resources 16 by Abingdon Press in 1987 and designed to be used by the presiding minister at the Lord's table. These texts include seasonal Great Thanksgivings, which can be prayed by the presiding minister while the people have in front of them either the brief text or the responses with cue lines. Also included are other ancient and contemporary Great Thanksgivings, which can be used if the people are supplied with the appropriate responses and cue lines.

Several musical settings for the people's responses are included in *The Upper Room Worshipbook* (pages 118-21), published by The Upper Room in 1985. Musical settings are also contained in the proposed *United Methodist Hymnal.*

By ancient tradition, the Great Thanksgiving is immediately followed by the Lord's Prayer, which should be prayed in unison. The people are called to pray the Lord's Prayer with these words: "And now, with the confidence of children of God, let us pray: . . . " These words are appropriate because the Great Thanksgiving has just reminded the people of all God's mighty acts whereby they are God's beloved children, and because they are about to address God as Father in the Lord's Prayer. The text printed with the services in *The Book of Services* is the ecumenical translation of the Lord's Prayer, prepared by the International Consultation on English Texts and now used by many denominations in the English-speaking world. Since the people in many congregations are accustomed to praying the Lord's Prayer in one of the two older translations used in the former Methodist and Evangelical United Brethren denominations respectively, all three translations are printed on pages 44-45 of *The Book of Services.* Congregations often pray the Lord's Prayer from memory in whatever translation they are accustomed to using.

d. Breaking the Bread

The breaking of bread is a gesture of invitation done in the name of the living Christ, the Head of his family and the Host at this meal. It can be done in such a way that persons immediately perceive its meaning, as when the minister, standing behind the Lord's table, lifts the unbroken loaf and in view of the people breaks it by hand. Even if individual wafers or pieces of bread are used, a large wafer or piece of bread or a symbolic loaf should be broken. If the minister cannot stand behind the table, the bread can at least be broken where the action can be seen by the people and perceived as a sign of invitation. After the bread has been broken, it is a natural gesture of invitation to raise the cup before the people.

These acts may be done in silence, or appropriate words may be spoken. Such words express a part, but only a part, of the rich symbolism of these gestures. Our unity in Christ, the message of distributive justice (bread for the world), the breaking of Jesus' body on the cross and the pouring out of his blood, and the Emmaus appearance when the risen Christ was recognized "in the breaking of the bread"—these are but a few of the possible meanings.

e. Giving the Bread and Cup

The giving of the bread and cup has traditionally been called the communion, which as we have seen is a translation of the New Testament Greek word *koinonia* in I Corinthians 10:16, which can also be translated "participation," "sharing," or "fellowship." Each of these translations adds a new dimension to the meanings of *koinonia* and of the act of giving and receiving the bread and cup.

This sharing is, of course, primarily nonverbal, but words are usually exchanged as the bread and cup are given and received. It is appropriate for the congregation to sing during the communion, thus reinforcing the communal nature of the celebration. Opportunity may be given for spontaneous song and praise.

The giving and receiving of the bread and cup can be done in various ways, depending on the size of the congregation and the design of the space in which they are worshiping.

Many congregations are accustomed to going forward in groups, kneeling at the rail in groups, receiving the bread and cup from the hands of the minister, and then being dismissed in groups. While many persons find this style meaningful, it can become an almost unbearably lengthy process when the congregation is large. To reduce the amount of time involved, additional ministers or laypersons can assist behind the rail in the serving of the bread and cup, and persons may come and go freely at the rail rather than being ushered to the rail by "tables."

Other congregations pass the bread and cup from hand to hand where they are seated. While this saves time, it has the serious disadvantage that the people are denied the opportunity to be active, to move forward rather than to sit passively and wait. Where this pattern is followed, the people should be encouraged to make the serving of the persons next to them a personal gesture of giving and receiving, perhaps spontaneously exchanging appropriate words. It is not necessary that all the people wait to eat or drink together at the same time.

An increasing number of congregations are finding that going forward, moving continuously past one or more places where the bread and cup are being given, and receiving communion standing combines advantages of receiving kneeling or seated. In this way, the people experience communion as *active*—active coming to receive and active going forth in the strength that communion gives. Persons may, if desired, be given the option of going to the rail immediately after receiving communion and kneeling there for as long as they wish.

At services where the congregation can stand gathered around the Lord's table, the people can easily and informally serve one another, with words exchanged as the Spirit moves.

However the bread and wine are distributed, two things should be clear. One is that the invitation is extended to all those present. The other is that persons who prefer not to receive should be able to refrain without embarrassment.

In any case, this giving and receiving should be a clear and powerful acting out of the gospel. It is God's self-giving to us through another person. For this reason, one person should serve another. Therefore, "self-service" communion, where persons go to the table or to the rail and help themselves to the bread and wine, should not be practiced, since it destroys the symbolism and power of the giving and receiving. Likewise, the practice of having the place of worship open over a period of time for persons to enter and leave as they wish, to take the elements without participating in the prayer and praise of the church, destroys the communal nature of the service and, therefore, is strongly discouraged.

When all have received, the remaining bread and wine are returned to the Lord's table, and it is set in order.

Here the symbolic power of what we do with the remaining bread and wine should not be underestimated. They may be set aside for distribution to the sick and others wishing communion but unable to attend. They may be reverently consumed by the minister(s) and others while the table is being put in order or following the service. They may be returned to the earth—a biblical gesture of worship (see II Samuel 23:16) and an ecological symbol today. Whatever we choose to do should express our stewardship of God's gifts and our respect for the purpose the bread and wine have served.

We have come to the end of the four basic actions at the Lord's table, but it is natural to wish to pause at this point for a brief prayer, thanking God for enabling us to share this holy meal and expressing the connection between our having received and our being sent to serve others as members of the body of Christ. A collection of such prayers is found on pages 45-46 of *The Book of Services.* Such a prayer may take the form of a hymn or hymn stanza, such as "Author of Life Divine," "For the Bread Which Thou Hast Broken," or the last two stanzas of "Here, O My Lord, I See Thee."

4. Sending Forth

Whether or not Holy Communion has been celebrated, the service concludes with a series of acts that are referred to as the Sending Forth. It is appropriate that the congregation stand for the Sending Forth.

A final hymn of sending forth seems just as fitting as an opening hymn of praise. It may be a hymn of thanksgiving and praise or of consecration to service in the world. It need not be an entire hymn, but may simply be one or more stanzas. In some circumstances, spontaneous song or spoken praise is appropriate. Many congregations sing a favorite hymn, song, stanza, or doxology at this point in every service. If Holy Communion has been celebrated, the closing hymn may simply be the sung prayer of thanksgiving after communion, mentioned above. If the congregation has been singing during the giving of the bread and cup, such a closing hymn could simply be the last of the hymns or songs sung.

If the final hymn is a recessional in which the pastor joins, it should follow the dismissal with blessing; otherwise, the dismissal with blessing follows the final hymn. In any case, the dismissal with blessing is prounounced in the name of God by the pastor to the people, face to face.

The church then goes forth to continue its service of God in the life of the world. Like the gathering, this going forth is an act of corporate worship while the people are still together in the place of worship. During this time, there may be organ or other instrumental music. The sharing of informal greetings, conversation, and fellowship following the dismissal with blessing is already customary in most United Methodist congregations and reflects the spirit of the peace.

CHAPTER II

The Calendar and Lectionary

Our weekly worship incorporates a balance between those things that are constant Sunday after Sunday and those that change. Finding the right balance of repetition and variety is crucial in planning effective worship. So far we have dealt with ways in which we structure that which remains constant; now we turn to the ways in which we structure change and variety.

We have seen that some items in the service remain constant and that others change from service to service. Chief among the latter are the hymns, psalms, scripture readings, sermon, and some of the prayers. These give variety to Christian worship, while the unchanging items give it stability.

Effective variety is not a chaotic succession of surprises; it needs to be structured just as surely as does stability. This need for structure does not at all rule out the unpredictable movings of the Spirit; indeed, we can respond more readily to such surprises if we experience them in a structured context. The Calendar of the Christian year, found on pages 50-51 of *The Book of Services*, is the basic pattern by which we structure variety in our worship.

Since ancient times, Christians have divided the day into hours, the week into days, and the year into days and seasons of special Christian significance. This "sanctification of time" not only gives Christian meaning to the hours, days, and seasons, but also is a way of encouraging, over a period of time, a balanced presentation of the various events in the history of salvation and the various emphases of Christian teaching. Through the centuries, while there has been much variation from time to time and from church to church, the Christian Calendar in its essentials is a unifying heritage.

Daily worship, with its sanctification of the hours, is a crucial part of our Christian heritage, which we are now seeking to recover. So much was involved in rightly recovering daily worship that it has become a major project of its own among United Methodists. When *The Book of Services* was being prepared for submission to the 1984 General Conference, the work on daily worship was at too early a stage to be included, and so this companion volume does not deal with it. Other publications, such as *The Upper Room Worshipbook*, have already appeared and *do* deal with daily worship, however, and much more is expected to be published in the next several years. Meanwhile, we have the Calendar of the Christian year in *The Book of Services*.

The most basic day in the Calendar is presupposed rather than explicitly listed. That day is the Lord's Day, Sunday, the first day of every week. On the first day of the week, God began the creation. On the eighth day, after resting on the seventh day, God resumed the ongoing work of creation. Above all, Christ was raised from the dead on the first day of the week, and on the first day of the week the Holy Spirit came upon the first Christians, and the Church was born. Indeed, every Lord's Day is a celebration of all God's mighty acts in Jesus Christ.

With few exceptions, the days listed in the Calendar are all Sundays—Lord's Days. The fact that a given day is the Lord's Day is even more important than the name given to that particular Lord's Day in the Christian year. No yearly celebration on any Sunday should be allowed to obscure the fact that it is the Lord's Day. Even in Lent, every Sunday is "a little Easter." Even more, Easter is a yearly great Sunday.

But as one Sunday follows another, we can't help asking, *"What* Sunday is this?" What Sunday in the year? What Sunday in the season? Confronted with the fact that we cannot fully proclaim every facet of the gospel every Sunday, we must ask, "What shall the service particularly focus on *this* Sunday?" As we go through the Sundays and other days of the Christian year, we are reminded of particular events in the saving work of Christ. We are pressed to make up our minds what we believe about Jesus Christ.

This calendar is the ecumenical Common Calendar, developed through the cooperative work of many Christian denominations. Developed as part of the same process was the ecumenical Common Lectionary, a three-year cycle of recommended scripture lessons and psalter selections now widely used in many denominations. Readers of this volume are urged to consult *Handbook of the Christian Year* (Abingdon, 1986), which contains a history of the origins and development of the Christian year, the story of how the Common Calendar and Lectionary were developed, the entire three-year Common Lectionary, a full explanation of the meaning of each of the days and seasons, and a collection of ideas and resources for celebrating each day and season.

The Christian year begins the First Sunday of Advent, which is the fourth Sunday before Christmas and always falls during the period November 27 through December 3. Advent focuses our attention on the past, present, and future comings of Christ so that we, too, may be a people prepared for his coming. We need no urging to celebrate Christmas, but why do our celebrations so often stop short the next day? The Epiphany is an older, and possibly even more profound, commemoration than Christmas and stresses the mystery of the manifestation of God in Jesus Christ. The word *epiphany* means "manifestation." The visit of the wise men, the baptism of the Lord, and the Transfiguration all deal with miraculous epiphanies. Thus the theme of Epiphany is echoed during the Season after Epiphany. These seasons collectively are known as the Christmas Cycle.

Even more important—the heart and center of the Christian year—is the Easter Cycle, which begins on Ash Wednesday, the first day of Lent. The season of Lent was originally the final period of preparation for those who were to be baptized at Easter, and it is also the time when those already baptized examine anew what it means to be a Christian and prepare for the renewal of their baptismal covenant at Easter. Holy Week, the climax of Lent, begins with Passion/Palm Sunday. It may seem strange that what we have commonly known as Palm Sunday is also Passion Sunday, but it makes excellent sense if we are to confront congregations today with what it means to be a follower of Christ.

Most persons who worship on Passion/Palm Sunday and on Easter do not attend the weekday services in between. To pass directly from the lesser triumph of the entry into Jerusalem to the greater triumph of the Resurrection without coming to terms with the passion that came between these two events would be to distort the gospel.

Even when Easter is experienced simply as a single hour of celebration, it is the high point of the Christian year. But it is much more than a single service. It concludes the Great Three Days—consisting of Holy Thursday evening, Good Friday, Holy Saturday, the Easter Vigil, and Easter morning. Those who observe these three days as a great unity experience the wholeness of what God has done for us in Christ. Furthermore, the Great Fifty Days from Easter through Pentecost constitute the Easter Season, the most important and joyous season of the Christian year.

These Great Fifty Days call for a fully trinitarian celebration. The forty days from Easter to Ascension commemorate the forty days of Jesus' resurrection appearances. The Great Fifty Days are also the season of creation and new creation, with origins in the ancient Jewish spring harvest season. This is the Pentecost Season, the season when the Holy Spirit breathed upon the disciples on the first Easter (John 20:19-23) and filled them on the day of Pentecost (Acts 2:1-4). The word *Pentecost* is, in fact, derived from the Greek word meaning "fifty days," which early Christians used for this season. This use of the term *Pentecost* can be confusing to United Methodists because in the recent past we had a summer Pentecost Season that *began* rather than ended with the day of Pentecost. On the other hand, an emphasis both on the risen Christ and on the Holy Spirit during the Great Fifty Days is not only ancient and ecumenical, but also appropriate to our experience, since it is only through the work of the Holy Spirit that we can know the risen Christ.

The whole second half of the year, following Pentecost, is known as the Season after Pentecost. It is *not* the Pentecost Season and does not have as its primary focus the work of the Holy Spirit. Its emphases are made evident Sunday by Sunday in the Lectionary readings. The Gospel readings for the Season after Pentecost go in course through the teaching portions of

Matthew (Year A), Mark (Year B), and Luke (Year C), in which Jesus' teachings about the kingdom of God are clearly central. This theme is sounded with particular strength on the last few Sundays after Pentecost and reaches a climax on the last Sunday, which is called Christ the King. For this reason, and because The United Methodist Church formerly had a fall season called Kingdomtide, the 1984 General Conference in adopting the Common Calendar specified that United Methodists who wish to do so may call this period Kingdomtide.

In addition to the days and seasons of the Christian year, churches commonly observe a variety of special days. Some of these are promoted by our denominational agencies and may involve special offerings. Other special days are observed by local or national custom. It is usually quite possible to observe these special days in appropriate ways while still observing the Christian year. It is important that the Calendar be seen not as a collection of special days but as a Christ-centered whole.

Churches that follow the Christian year commonly use distinctive symbols and colors to announce what day or season it is. Paraments, stoles, and banners lend themselves to such use. Many suggestions and alternatives are found in *Handbook of the Christian Year*. These are not matters of church law, and customs have varied widely from one time and place to another.

Many local churches, however, feel the need of a simple system of colors to symbolize the days and seasons of the Christian year—a system not cluttered with alternatives. Here is such a system, based on the principle of purple for preparatory seasons, white for festival seasons, and green for an "ordinary time" of growth.

ADVENT — purple
CHRISTMAS — white
SEASON AFTER EPIPHANY — green, except for white on the first and last Sundays (Baptism of the Lord and Transfiguration Sunday)
LENT — purple, except perhaps white on Holy Thursday and no color at all on Good Friday and Holy Saturday

EASTER SEASON — white, except for red on the Day of Pentecost
SEASON AFTER PENTECOST — green, except for white on the first and last Sundays (Trinity Sunday and Christ the King) and All Saints

These are the basic, or background, colors, but it should be remembered that most visuals contain two or more colors. For example, the festive colors of gold and red are often used with white during the Christmas and Easter Seasons.

Red has a variety of special uses. As the color of fire, symbolizing the Holy Spirit, it is used not only on the day of Pentecost, but also for ordinations and consecrations. A deep hue of red symbolizes the blood of Christ and is often used during Holy Week, beginning with Passion/Palm Sunday, and when martyrs are being commemorated. Red is also appropriate for evangelistic services, for anniversaries and homecomings, and for civil observances, such as Thanksgiving.

CHAPTER III

The Baptismal Covenant

A. Introduction to the Service

1. The Nature of Baptism

Baptism is an outward sign of our new life in Jesus Christ. Through the sacrament of baptism, God declares that he has adopted us as his children, making us fellow heirs of God's riches (Galatians 4:4-7, Romans 8:14-17). Or, to use another New Testament metaphor, God declares that we are citizens of Christ's kingdom—"a royal priesthood, a holy nation" (I Peter 2:9).

Baptism is a means God uses to assure us that we are no longer strangers or visitors to God's kingdom, but rather fellow citizens with the saints and members of God's household, the foundation of which is the apostles and prophets with Christ himself as the chief cornerstone (Ephesians 2:19-20). Hence this sacrament of initiation into the Christian faith is not a minor and insignificant rite of the Church; instead, it is a visible way of proclaiming the gospel. The good news has to do both with God's active grace on our behalf and our active response to God.

God brings us into the family of Christ by his own action. Jesus reminded his disciples that they had not chosen him but were chosen by him (John 15:16), for it is God who calls and saves us. Our entrance into the Christian family through baptism is an indication that we do not become God's people because we are deserving but because God is gracious.

God's love revealed in the sacrament of entrance is the same

love that has been at work from the beginning of time. Through
the physical element of baptismal water, God presents to us the
story of eternal, saving love. God brings to our attention his first
action in the creation of the world: God moved across the dark
waters of chaos and called forth light. Through the water of the
sacrament, God also reminds us that in the time of Noah he called
into the ark a remnant of his creation, thus saving his living
creatures from destruction by the water. God further reminds us
in baptism that he called his enslaved people out of Egypt and in
the Exodus led them through the water of the sea to freedom.

Numerous other biblical stories tell of God's saving action in
the presence of water; all of these are brought to mind in baptism,
but none so strongly as Creation, Flood, and Exodus. The water
of initiation presents to us our heritage, the story of the family we
join by divine grace. This story culminates in Jesus Christ, who is
the head of God's family, the Church. Jesus was himself baptized
by John. At Jesus' baptism, he received the assurance of God's
love: "You are my beloved Son" (Mark 1:11). Jesus Christ is
God's Son by nature; we are made God's children by adoption.
What unites us is the divine love that permeates everything.

There is another side to be considered. The good news involves
not only God's active grace on our behalf, but also our active
response to God. When we are called into God's fellowship, we
are also commissioned to serve God. Our status as children of
God and as citizens of the kingdom does not bestow on us special
privileges; on the contrary, it places on us special responsibilities.
Jesus told his disciples not only that he had chosen them, but also
that he had appointed them to "go and bear fruit" and "to love one
another" (John 15:16, 17).

Because God is gracious, he seeks the salvation of all his
people, not just some of them. To those who have received God's
saving love through faith, he gives the task of seeking out others,
sharing the good news, and living in righteousness with all people.
Through baptism, God reveals what he expects of us as well as
what he does for us. We respond in love.

Baptism, therefore, is a covenant. In the biblical tradition, God
binds himself to his people through a covenant promise; those
who are bound to God respond by promising to be faithful. But
there is not a separate or individual covenant made afresh each

time the sacrament is administered; rather, the baptismal covenant is an expression and indication of God's covenant, which Christ sealed with his own sacrifice (Hebrews 9:11-22). Baptism is not a contract that God negotiates with each person separately according to the whim or circumstances of the moment; baptism is an affirmation of what God has done for all of us in Jesus Christ. Through the sacrament, God gives us the assurance that the promise of the universal covenant applies to us personally, and we accept our responsibility to participate in the covenant obligations together with all other Christians. All that God promises is ours as part of God's people.

Because of the nature of this covenant, we are united not only to God but also to his whole Church. We are also united to a particular congregational unit of that Church. We are not initiated merely into a denomination; we are made members of Christ's holy Church. Differences of opinion and practice among Christians are differences within the family, not differences among unrelated families. All who trust in Christ are our brothers and sisters in the faith. The visible expression of this corporate nature of the Church is the local community of faith. A specific congregation of Christians is a representative of the whole Church and is the fellowship within which we grow and work. Therefore, the presence of the congregation at the time of the administration of the sacrament is important as an expression of this reality.

The practice of baptizing infants and children grows out of the covenantal nature of the sacrament. The baptism of those who cannot yet outwardly respond is a potent reminder to the whole Church that God initiates the covenant. As Paul reminded the Romans, God reached out to us and acted in Christ "while we were yet helpless" (Romans 5:6). Our obedience to God is a response to God's love freely offered to us; we do not serve God in order to earn his love.

At the same time, the initiation of those who cannot yet make a profession of faith emphasizes the corporate nature and responsibility of the covenant people. Always the congregation takes the responsibility for the nurture and support of the newly baptized, but when these persons are infants or children, the necessity of providing opportunities for growth and fellowship is more apparent. Thus the community is reminded of its obligation.

The baptism of infants and children can occur only within the covenant framework. Missionaries cannot go into an area where there is no Christian congregation and begin baptizing babies, but once a congregation of believers is established, the children of the faithful are not to be regarded as little pagans until they attain a certain age of enlightenment and spiritual insight. Rather, they are to be seen as heirs of the covenant; the statement of Peter on the day of Pentecost that "the promise is to you and to your children" is an important insight into the nature of the covenant community (Acts 2:39). The Church provides the spiritual home within which children learn the meaning of their baptism and are given opportunities to respond in faith.

Traditionally there have been three ways in which baptism is administered; each indicates something of value about the nature of the sacrament. Immersion is a symbol of burial and resurrection and a reminder that we have been buried with Christ in baptism in order that we might be raised to walk in newness of life (Romans 6:3-4). The pouring of water upon those being baptized signifies the New Testament gift of the Holy Spirit to the Church, recalling the words of Joel: "I will pour out my spirit on all flesh" (Joel 2:28, cf. Acts 2:17). Sprinkling is a reminder that in Christ God has fulfilled the promise announced by Ezekiel: "I will sprinkle clean water upon you, and you shall be clean from all your uncleanness. . . . A new heart I will give you, and a new spirit I will put within you; and I will take out of your flesh the heart of stone and give you a heart of flesh" (Ezekiel 36:25-26). Although only one manner of baptism is used on a particular occasion, all three taken together witness to the nature of the sacrament: God cleanses us from sin and brings us to newness of life through the death and resurrection of Christ; by the power of the Holy Spirit, God puts within us a new heart that we may serve him faithfully. Through baptism, God's active grace on our behalf calls forth our active response to God in a covenant of faith.

The biblical act of the laying on of hands, signifying the action of the Holy Spirit, has followed the act of baptism with water and been part of the total baptismal action since ancient times. During much of our history, this act was separated in time from baptism and delayed until confirmation. It is, of course, also traditional on such other occasions as ordinations and healing services. Our new service restores the ancient practice of laying on hands as part of the service of baptism. At the same time, it is recognized that the laying on of hands, unlike baptism itself, is repeatable and is also appropriately done at confirmation, reaffirmations of faith, and other occasions, such as ordinations and healing services. Indeed, one of the functions of laying on hands at these later services is to act as a reminder that we have been baptized and that these later acts have their basis in the baptismal covenant.

2. Baptism in Relation to Confirmation and Reaffirmation of Faith

Since baptism is first of all God's promise to us that we are a part of God's family, the sacrament is administered only once to each person, for the promises of God are trustworthy, and birth or adoption into a family occurs but once. To ask that God should repeat his sacramental promise is to cast doubt on God's word and on our status as God's people.

Nevertheless there are occasions when doubts will arise within us about our relationship to God, and there are occasions when God's love is experienced with such new warmth and clarity that some public testimony of God's grace is desired and appropriate. At such times it is possible to affirm the baptismal covenant. In this act of affirmation, we are reminded of what God has faithfully promised, and we affirm our own commitment to God.

For those who have been baptized as infants or children, there is a significant first occurrence of such affirmation, commonly called "confirmation." The title is appropriate on three counts: First, in this rite, God confirms his promise to those who were too young to understand that promise at the time of their baptism. Second, these persons confirm their personal commitment in a public testimony they were unable to make as infants or children. Third, the congregation confirms the commitment they made at baptism to be a nurturing and supportive community of faith to those who are now being confirmed. Through this triple confirmation, faith and dedication are strengthened.

Two unfortunate practices have grown up with respect to confirmation, however, and both need careful examination. First, it has been assumed that even those being baptized as youths or adults must participate in the rite of confirmation in order to make a full profession of faith. Thus it has frequently happened that on the same day persons had been baptized (or only a few days later) they were also asked to reaffirm their baptismal vows. At best, such practices involve needless duplication; at worst, they violate the integrity of the baptismal rite itself. Therefore, when persons are baptized as youths or adults, no separate act of confirmation is necessary or desirable.

One exception should be noted. When someone has received baptism outside of a congregational service of worship because of exceptional circumstances, it is appropriate that as soon as possible this person should make a public affirmation in the presence of the congregation; this affirmation could take the form of the confirmation rite.

The second unfortunate practice concerning confirmation grows out of the assumption that the baptismal covenant should be affirmed only once during an entire lifetime. While the first affirmation of faith by those baptized in infancy is extremely important, its importance should not blind us to the need for reaffirmation at other times. Although God does not forget his promises to us, we do tend to forget them, and in times of stress we may doubt the truth of God's promises even if we do not forget their existence. Furthermore, we frequently neglect the obligations placed upon us in the baptismal covenant. For these reasons, it is appropriate for every Christian to reaffirm the baptismal covenant from time to time.

For the sake of clarity and tradition, the term *confirmation* should be reserved for the first profession of the baptismal faith made by those who received the sacrament during infancy or childhood. To this historic rite, however, two other categories should be added: individual reaffirmation (on the part of specific individuals) and congregational reaffirmation (by the entire worshiping assembly of baptized persons).

Individual reaffirmation can occur for a variety of reasons. For example: (1) Those who have not taken their baptismal obligations seriously may wish to reaffirm their commitment; this has usually been called "reaffirmation of faith." (2) Persons transferring membership into a congregation, whether from another United Methodist congregation or from another denomination, may wish to make a public testimony to their faith in the presence of the congregation to which they come. Such a reaffirmation discounts neither their membership status nor their personal commitment prior to this time. It does provide an opportunity for witness not available in the mere presentation of a formal letter of transfer. (3) Similarly, persons establishing affiliate or associate membership in a congregation may be encouraged to make their faith known through a service of reaffirmation. (4) Frequently some form of public testimony and thanksgiving is desired by persons who have reached a new level of commitment or a heightened awareness of God's grace through an experience such as conversion, rededication of life, healing, or an awareness of the work of the Holy Spirit. Since all such experiences grow out of the very grace that baptism signifies, it is particularly fitting that these persons should reaffirm the baptismal covenant in the presence of the congregation.

The other category, congregational reaffirmation, involves all baptized persons present in the worshiping community. A congregation has an opportunity to reaffirm its baptismal faith each time the sacrament of baptism is administered in its midst. For this reason, congregational participation in the baptismal service is important, particularly in the vows affirming our Christian faith. Congregations should be aware that at the same time God declares his promise to individuals being baptized, God is reminding those already baptized of the promise he has given them in the sacrament. But it is also fitting for an act of congregational reaffirmation to occur at appropriate times even when there is no candidate to be baptized.

Two occasions in the Christian year particularly lend themselves to congregational reaffirmation of the baptismal covenant: (1) the Easter Vigil or another time within the season of Easter, such as Pentecost, and (2) the Sunday after the Epiphany (January 6), which is the Sunday of the Baptism of the Lord. Easter is an appropriate occasion, since through the sacrament we die and are buried with Christ in order that we might be raised with Christ to new life. At Easter there is particular emphasis on the Exodus theme, because Jesus' death and resurrection occurred at Passover, and early Christians understood Jesus to be the new Moses who leads his people out of the slavery of sin and death. The Baptism of the Lord is also an appropriate time, since it recalls the baptism of Jesus in the Jordan. The renewal theme is reinforced by the fact that this occasion falls at the beginning of the secular calendar year, a natural period for self-examination and renewed commitment to tasks ahead. The Wesleyan tradition of a covenant service at the beginning of the new year makes this time seem especially appropriate to many United Methodists. In addition, there are other times in the year, such as All Saints, in which reaffirmation of the baptismal covenant is appropriate.

Reception into The United Methodist Church as a society (in the Wesleyan sense of the word) within Christ's universal Church and reception into a local congregation have in Wesleyan tradition been closely related to baptism and confirmation and are appropriately included with the services of the baptismal covenant. It is not enough that persons being baptized and confirmed be received as "generic Christians" into the universal Church; they need to belong to a particular community of faith that will nurture them and in whose mission they can participate by their prayers, their presence, their gifts, and their service.

B. Commentary on the Text

1. Preliminary Rubrics

The heading of the text states that this service "is to be included where possible in a service of public worship, preferably as a response to the proclamation of the Word." It is not an independent service that can stand alone, and it assumes the presence of the worshiping congregation. As the commentary on Services of Word and Table has already made clear (see above, pages 55–56), its appropriate place in the Sunday service is as a response to the Word.

Both the preface "Concerning Services of the Baptismal Covenant" and the opening rubric give this service a great deal of flexibility and assume a great deal of pastoral discretion. This is necessary because there are so many different occasions where this service is called for, including:

1. The baptism of infants and children.
2. The baptism of youth and adults.
3. Confirmation.
4. Individual reaffirmation of faith.
5. Reception of members from another denomination.
6. Reception of members from other United Methodist churches.
7. Congregational reaffirmation of the baptismal covenant.
8. Combinations of the above occasions.

As the preface points out, combinations of these occasions are very common, often even the norm, and there are so many possible combinations that there is simply no way to print out a separate service tailored to each situation that a pastor may encounter.

It is also true that any one of these acts may vary in its requirements from one local church or one occasion to another. Where possible, it is highly effective to have a group of baptisms, confirmations, and/or receptions as a high festival occasion, which becomes the focus for the whole Sunday service that day. Easter, Pentecost, Baptism of the Lord, and All Saints are particularly appropriate occasions for such a baptismal festival. In some small congregations, even a single baptism or confirmation may be a rare and special occasion. On the other hand, in very large or rapidly growing congregations there may be one or more of the above acts every Sunday, and it may be quite unfeasible to make such acts the focus of the whole service. Thus circumstances may indicate that any one of these acts may be celebrated in all its fullness or shortened as may be necessary.

Since *The Book of Services* has been published, many persons, while appreciating the flexibility of the service, have expressed the desire for specific indications as to what parts of the service are to be used on what occasions. For this reason, as each part of the service is discussed, it will be indicated when that part of the service is to be used, is optional, or is not to be used.

2. Introduction to the Service

The Introduction is used without the final paragraph when there are *only* baptisms. The whole Introduction is used when there are confirmations or reaffirmations of faith. If there is *only* reception of members into the congregation, without reaffirmation of faith, the Introduction may be omitted.

Persons being baptized or confirmed or individually reaffirming their faith (together with their parents or sponsors, if any) assemble near the font before this introduction is read. They may be joined by other family members and representatives of the congregation. Where the space and the size of the congregation permit, the entire congregation may gather with the candidates.

3. Presentation of Candidates

Persons are presented for baptism, confirmation, or reaffirmation of faith. When candidates for baptism are infants or children, both their names and the names of their parents and sponsors may be mentioned. [Example: "I present Jean Ann, daughter of Mary and Allen Smith, for baptism."]

Persons being received into the congregation without reaffirmation of faith are presented here or immediately before they are received.

If there is *only* reception of members into the congregation without reaffirmation of faith, everything between the Presentation and the Reception into The United Methodist Church or Reception into the Local Congregation is omitted.

If there is *only* a congregational reaffirmation of the baptismal covenant there are, of course, no presentations.

The presentation may be made by the lay leader or other representative of the congregation designated for this responsibility.

4. Renunciation of Sin and Profession of Faith

These questions and answers are used *unless* there is *only* reception of members into the congregation without reaffirmation of faith. The fourth question and answer are used *only* when there are candidates not able to answer for themselves. The fifth question and answer are used *only* when there are candidates able to answer for themselves and when there is a congregational reaffirmation of the baptismal covenant.

These questions are addressed to, and answered by, parents and/or sponsors when persons being baptized are too young or too incapacitated by a handicapping condition to answer for themselves. Children are normally sponsored by their parent(s), but in some situations other persons serve as sponsors in addition to, or even instead of, the parent(s).

While it is not necessary to have sponsors for persons who are able to answer for themselves, congregations may elect to provide individual sponsors for them. The portion of the fifth question within brackets [ ] is added when there are such sponsors.

In addition to the role of parents or other individual sponsors, the whole congregation assumes a sponsoring role, expressed as the people answer the question addressed to the congregation and join in the Apostles' Creed. In trial versions of this service, the congregation was asked to assume this role by taking the vows in unison with the sponsors and candidates, but testing indicated that congregations understood their sponsoring role better if they answered a special question addressed to them as a congregation.

It is appropriate for the worshipers to rise for the Renunciation and Profession and to remain standing through the end of the Thanksgiving over the Water.

The full text of the profession of faith is the Apostles' Creed in question-and-answer form. This creed, in its most ancient form, was designed to be used in this way on the occasion of baptism. When pastoral considerations make it necessary, the material in brackets [ ] may be omitted. Although the shorter answers fulfill the requirements of *The Book of Discipline*, the full text is a desirable expression of the historic and universal faith of the Christian Church.

5. Thanksgiving over the Water

This is used whenever water is used either for baptism or for the remembrance of baptism.

Water may be poured into the baptismal font just prior to this prayer. An ample quantity of water should be used, and silence observed, in order that the congregation may both see and hear the water as it flows into the font. This action helps Christians appreciate the gracious use God makes of the physical world, for it is in the nature of sacraments to reveal God's love through the use of material substances that appeal to our senses.

Congregational participation in the responses is urged. Where it is not feasible for the congregation to join in the responses, the following adaptation should be made. (1) Omit the opening dialogue ("The Lord be with you." **"And also with you."**) if it is not already familiar to the congregation. (2) Omit the two responses, **"Sing to the Lord. . . . "** and **"Declare his works. . . ."** (3) Retain the final response (**"All praise to you. . . ."**), spoken by the minister, since it forms the conclusion of the prayer.

6. *Baptism with Laying on of Hands*

This is used only when there are persons to be baptized.

The traditional question, "What name is given this child?" is omitted in this service. The child's name has already been spoken at the time of the Presentation of Candidates. This change reflects our current cultural situation, in which children are named within hours of birth, but usually are not presented for baptism until weeks later. Since children come to the font having names, it is not appropriate to pretend that they are given their names at the font. If, however, the family wishes to follow the traditional custom, or if there is a large number of children and the minister needs to be reminded of each child's name, the traditional question may quietly be asked and answered.

The given name of the candidate is spoken as a part of the baptismal formula. The surname should not be included.

In the act of baptism, a generous quantity of water should be used. Since baptism is a sign of God's generous love, and since the physical elements used in sacraments are intended to reveal this love to us through our senses, it is important that the congregation be able to see the baptismal action and that the water be seen, heard, and felt, regardless of the mode of baptism being employed.

Immediately following the baptism of each candidate with water is the laying on of hands. If there is more than one candidate, the laying on of hands takes place before the minister baptizes the next candidate. On the other hand, the minister should not combine the two acts by simply laying a wet hand on the candidate's head. The acts of baptism with water and the laying on of hands are separate acts, each with its own biblical and historic significance.

Others may join the minister in laying hands on the newly baptized. These may include parents and other family members, sponsors, the lay leader or other representative who has presented the candidate, and others who may be gathered at the font. In particular, when the family includes baptized children, these children should be encouraged to share in the act.

Several optional acts may be inserted into the service immediately following the act of Baptism with Laying on of Hands. The minister may trace on the forehead of the baptized person the sign of the cross. This may be done in silence or with the words, "*(Name)*, [child of God], you are sealed by the Holy Spirit in baptism and marked as Christ's own forever." Olive oil may be used in this action, following the biblical custom of anointing persons with oil in holy rites. Such anointing is a reminder that through baptism we are made a part of the priesthood of all believers.

New clothing is sometimes presented to those just baptized, particularly in the case of infants, as a symbol of the new life we have in Christ. Words such as these may be used: "Receive these new clothes as a token of the new life that is given in Christ Jesus."

A lighted baptismal candle may also be presented to the newly baptized person or to the sponsors, with the use of such words as these: "Let your light so shine that *others*, seeing your good works, may glorify our Father in heaven." When the candle is presented to the parents or sponsors of children, *"others"* may be changed to "this child" or "these children." A baptismal candle bears either a Christian symbol or no decoration at all; it should not be confused with ornate "birthday candles" sold commercially to mark off the child's birthdays annually. On the other hand, it is appropriate to light the baptismal candle in the home each year on the anniversary of baptism as a reminder of the grace of God offered through baptism.

If the congregation uses a Paschal candle during the Easter Season, this is relighted at baptisms and stands near the font. The baptismal candle is then lighted from the Paschal candle. Otherwise the baptismal candle may be lighted from one of the candles on or near the Lord's table.

If more than one of these optional acts is used, it is suggested that they be done in the order given above.

While these optional acts can increase the awareness of the rich meanings in the sacrament of baptism, care should be taken not to let them overshadow the act of baptism itself. Always the use of oil, new clothes, and baptismal candles is secondary to God's sign given in the water itself.

Another option is to give opportunity for those who have received baptism or confirmation or who have been received from another congregation to bear witness to their faith or experience in their own words. Whether such opportunity is extended or not will depend on factors such as the number of persons, the amount of time available, the nature of the congregation, and the background and experience of the persons to whom the opportunity is extended. Such oral testimony may be inserted into the service at any appropriate point, perhaps immediately before the Commendation and Welcome.

7. Confirmation or Reaffirmation of Faith

The words, "Remember your baptism and be thankful," are used not only when individuals are being confirmed or reaffirming their faith, but also when the entire congregation is reaffirming the baptismal covenant.

The use of water is optional. If it is sprinkled toward individuals being confirmed or reaffirming their faith, or toward the congregation, the quantity should be small, as this act is intended only as a reminder of baptism. It is most important that it not create the impression of being "rebaptism." For the same reason, the rubric indicates that "water may be sprinkled *toward* those being confirmed or reaffirming their faith," not falling directly upon their heads as would be the case in baptism by sprinkling. The sprinkling may be done by dipping the end of a small evergreen branch in the font, or in a bowl of water carried from the font, and shaking it toward the person or congregation. This may be seen as representing biblical sprinkling with hyssop for purification (Exodus 12:22, Psalm 51:7, etc.). Another possible way of using water is for the minister to scoop up a handful of water from the font, high enough for the congregation to see the water, and then let it fall back into the font so that the congregation can hear it splash, while saying, "Remember your baptism and be thankful."

The placing of hands on the head of each person separately, with the words "*(Name)*, the Holy Spirit works within you . . . " is done only when there are individuals presenting themselves for confirmation or reaffirmation of faith. These words are similar to those used immediately after baptism, but the differences that do exist between the two indicate an important theological understanding: Baptism is the beginning that cannot be repeated; in later acts, God continues what was begun in Baptism. As in Baptism, only the given name of the candidate is used, and others may join the minister in the laying on of hands if desired.

If water is to be sprinkled toward the congregation on an occasion where individuals are being confirmed or reaffirming their faith, this may be done *after* the laying on of hands.

8. *Profession or Renewal of Membership in The United Methodist Church*

This is used when persons are baptized on their own profession of faith, or are confirmed, or reaffirm their faith individually or as a congregation.

The first of the two questions, concerning loyalty to The United Methodist Church, is also used with persons joining the congregation (and The United Methodist Church) from another denomination. If such persons have not been presented earlier in the service, they may be presented at this time. If such persons do not reaffirm their faith, and if there are no baptisms, confirmations, or other reaffirmations of faith, the service may begin with the Presentation and this Profession.

Persons being received into associate membership, whose primary membership is in a congregation of another denomination, may wish to use the following modified form of the first question: "As *members* of Christ's universal Church and of *(other denomination's name),* will you work within The United Methodist Church and do all in your power to strengthen its ministries?"

The second question, concerning membership in the local congregation, is also used when persons are joining the congregation either from another denomination or from another United Methodist congregation. If there are persons joining the congregation from other United Methodist congregations who have not been presented earlier in the service, they may be presented immediately before the asking of this second question. If on a particular occasion there are *only* persons joining on transfer from another United Methodist congregation, the service may begin with the Presentation and this second question.

For persons being received into associate membership, whose primary membership is in another congregation, the second question may begin: "As associate members (an associate member) of this congregation, will you faithfully participate in its ministries . . . ?" For a mixed group of persons being received, some into full membership and some into associate membership in the congregation, the question may begin: "As members or associate members of this congregation, . . . ?"

9. Commendation and Welcome

This is used in all cases, but when there is *only* a congregational reaffirmation of the baptismal covenant, it should be adapted by omitting the minister's commendation ("Members of the household of God. . . . ") and changing the unison prayer of thanksgiving to begin: "We give thanks for all that God has already given us. As members of the body of Christ. . . . "

When infants and children have been baptized, it should be understood that both they and their sponsors are being commended and welcomed.

The closing rubrics provide that this service may be followed by acts and words of welcome and peace, appropriate thanksgivings and intercessions, and Holy Communion.

The traditional unity of Word and Sacrament should be maintained. While it is not intended that the minister preach on the meaning of these rites each time they are administered, ample provision should be made in the preaching program to instruct congregations in the meaning of these rites and the nature of the baptismal covenant. It is most fitting that services that include these rites conclude with Holy Communion, in which the union of the new members with the body of Christ is most fully expressed.

C. General Instructions

1. Responsible Sacramental Discipline

The United Methodist Church recognizes all Christian baptism, regardless of the age at which it was administered, the mode employed, or the denominational affiliation of the person administering the rite. When a person is known to have been baptized previously, it is imperative that the sacrament not be repeated. "Rebaptism" calls into doubt the promise God extended at the reception of the sacrament. It also calls into question our respect for other Christian churches and ministers and betrays a lack of concern for the unity of Christ's holy Church through baptism.

If there is uncertainty as to whether a person has been baptized, and if neither records nor witnesses can be found, baptism may be administered conditionally using these words: "*(Name)*, if you are not already baptized, I baptize you in the name of the Father and of the Son and of the Holy Spirit." **"Amen."**

Administration of the sacrament should be preceded by prebaptismal instruction for candidates and their parents and other sponsors. Congregations are encouraged to provide study groups and other corporate counseling opportunities in addition to individual consultations by the pastor.

Pastors are urged to exercise responsible sacramental discipline. Baptism may be justifiably deferred or declined when those seeking the rite will not participate in prebaptismal counseling, or when parents or other sponsors proposed for infants and children are not themselves committed members of Christ's Church. The vows taken by parents and sponsors in baptism plainly presuppose their Christian commitment.

A pastor should also defer baptizing anyone who has been refused this rite by another Christian pastor until the latter has been contacted and reasons for the refusal have been ascertained and evaluated.

2. The Presence of the Congregation

Baptism is to be administered in the presence of the congregation of which the candidate will be an active member. Pastors are urged to deny requests for private baptismal services, whether held in the church building or elsewhere. Persons who are presently related to a particular local church but request baptism in another local church for reasons of sentiment should be referred to their own congregations and pastors for the rite.

On rare occasions, emergency baptism may be pastorally justified if those requesting it urgently need outward and visible reassurance of God's grace. When someone is baptized outside of congregational worship, an announcement of the fact should be made at the next Sunday service. Persons who recover from illness after emergency baptism should be presented to the local congregation; at such times, the rite of reaffirmation may be appropriate. In any event, the Commendation and Welcome should be included. Any persons receiving emergency baptism should later receive the benefit of the counseling that normally would precede the rite.

Congregations holding two or more services a Sunday should find ways of informing the whole congregation concerning baptisms, confirmations, and reception of members from other congregations. Such acts at an early service should be announced at the later service(s), and such acts as are anticipated at a later service should be announced at the earlier service(s). The persons involved can be prayed for during the intercessions. If this is not possible, at least announcement can be printed in the congregational newsletter or bulletin the following week.

3. The Baptismal Font

Specific suggestions regarding the placement of the font are hard to make because of the variety of church architecture that exists, but several principles can be stated. (1) The font should be in as full a view of the entire congregation as possible. (2) The font should be placed where a group of persons can gather around or in front of it for the administration of the sacrament. (3) The font should always be present in the place of worship as a visible reminder of the centrality of this sacrament and should not be stored in a closet or relegated to an obscure position when baptism is not being administered. (4) The font should be of substantial size, reflecting the importance of Holy Baptism.

The font should include a bowl or basin large enough to hold a generous amount of water. When sprinkling or pouring, the water may be administered with the hand or with the traditional baptismal shell. When the mode is immersion and there is no suitable baptismal pool in the church building, the service may be held out of doors or in the baptismal pool of a neighboring church; members of the candidate's congregation should be encouraged to attend such special services. Where requests for immersion are frequent, this fact should be taken into consideration when church buildings are being designed or renovated, in order that facilities for immersion may be provided in the place where the congregation worships.

CHAPTER IV

A Service of Christian Marriage

A. Introduction to the Service

1. A Complete Service of Worship

A new Service of Christian Marriage for United Methodists results from a renewed and reformed understanding of worship and of the theology of Christian marriage. This renewal in turn arises from an ongoing study of the scriptures, the traditions of the universal Church, the practices of our own denomination, and the manifold claims of our modern times. Each of these roots of renewal, taken separately and together, confirms that something more profound and substantial is required than revising the text or modernizing the language of what has been the Order for the Service of Marriage, adopted by the 1964 Methodist General Conference and contained in *The Book of Worship* (1965).

As *The Book of Services* indicates in the preface "Concerning a Service of Christian Marriage," the new service is distinctive in several crucial respects: (1) It is a service of Christian worship that sets the marriage rite in the context of a Service of the Word and provides the option of Holy Communion. (2) It involves those present as an active congregation rather than simply as passive witnesses. (3) Both words and actions consistently reflect the belief that husband and wife are entering of their own volition and as equal partners into a holy covenant reflecting Christ's baptismal covenant with the Church.

Traditional as the 1964 Order may seem in text and theology, it is not a complete service of Word and Sacrament. It does not indicate in the rubrics how it might be ordered and celebrated as such. While the Order has included prayers, and in its 1964 revision suggests the singing of hymns, it lacks scripture and is plainly not a Service of the Word. While it rightly points out possible abuses when Holy Communion is celebrated, it needlessly discourages Holy Communion on occasions when the sacrament would be appropriate.

The 1964 Order reflects its medieval origins as an ecclesiastical solemnization of the marriage contract. The essence of our familiar marriage vows (" . . . to have and to hold, from this day forward. . . . ") conveys the ancient sense of a legal contract freely consented to before witnesses.

The opening address in the 1964 Order still contains the remnant of a bann, which was originally to be read or published on three Sundays previous to the date of the marriage. In the absence of a complete service of worship, betrothal and nuptial vows sound like legal requirements for a contract. The prayers and religious language in the other parts of the traditional order tend to become a mixture of invocations and moral injunctions, rather than ordered elements in an act of worship.

During John Wesley's lifetime, it was illegal for persons to be married in any church or chapel except those of the established Church of England.[1] For this reason, and because Wesley was a priest who loved *The Book of Common Prayer*, he adopted its rite of marriage when he prepared his 1784 service book for American Methodists. He deleted the ring ceremony, perhaps because of scruples about wearing ornaments and jewelry. He also omitted the act of giving the woman in marriage. American Methodists later made other changes, such as omitting the betrothal vows. In the later nineteenth and early twentieth centuries, these ceremonies were restored. After 1864 in the Methodist Episcopal Church the woman's promise to "obey" and "serve" her husband was omitted. Nonetheless, the basic structure and text of the 1964 Order are still very similar to "The Forme of Solemnizacion of Matrimonie" in Thomas Cranmer's 1549 *Book of Common Prayer*. Much of Cranmer's work was based on the Latin rite of Sarum (Salisbury). The lovely wedding vows predate the Reformation by more than a century and were said by the couple in English long before the rest of the rite was translated from Latin.

In recent years, there has been a growing conviction that the solemnization of marriage for Christians should be a public service of worship. This can be seen in the changes of the title and location of this rite in "The Ritual" during the past two hundred years. After Wesley's 1784 service book was abandoned by American Methodists in 1792, the marriage rite was placed with the other rites in the back of *The Doctrines and Discipline of the Methodist Episcopal Church*, still entitled "The Form of Solemnization of Matrimony." During the nineteenth century, it was often grouped with the occasional services, and the "Form" became the "Order" for the Solemnization of Matrimony. In the 1965 edition of *The Book of Worship*, it was included among the "General Services of the Church," and its archaic title changed to "The Order for the Service of Marriage."

All the major traditions and churches have revised or newly written marriage services in recent years. These have been carefully studied, and our new United Methodist "Service of Christian Marriage" is indebted to this work in the universal Church. The underlying reason for a new United Methodist rite is the same as that for other churches. "We seek to give liturgical expression to a view of Christian marriage and of the relationship between the sexes which incorporates modern insights and which differs . . . from that of earlier periods."[2]

2. The Theology of Marriage

The institution of marriage is based on the order of creation. The preface to the earliest (1549) edition of *The Book of Common Prayer* refers to "holy matrimony [as] an honorable estate instituted of God in paradise."[3] "So God created man in his own image, in the image of God he created them; male and female he created them" (Genesis 1:27). In spite of the fact that most Bible translations of this passage still use the words *man, he,* and *his,* it is plain that males and females are equally created in the image of God. Jesus recalled this created equality in his teaching on divorce: "But from the beginning of the creation, 'God made them male and female' " (Mark 10:6).

The equality of male and female is clearly stated in such passages as Paul's declaration: "For as many of you as were baptized into Christ have put on Christ. There is neither Jew nor Greek, there is neither slave nor free, there is neither male nor female; for you are all one in Christ Jesus" (Galatians 3:27-28). This understanding of the equality of the sexes governs our reading of those passages of scripture which seemingly or actually reflect a culturally conditioned patriarchal view.

Christian marriage is a sign of a lifelong covenant between a man and a woman. They fulfill each other, and their love gives birth to new life *in* each and *through* each. This union of love is possible because Christ is the bond of unity. He is this bond of unity when both their lives are centered in him. Paul writes the Ephesians: "Be subject to one another out of reverence for Christ" (5:21). Paul's whole discussion makes sense only in the light of that basic and mutual bond between spouses *and* Christ.

Christian marriage confirms this grace-filled *equality* of female and male in Christ. When a man and a woman are baptized into Christ, they also discover their *uniqueness* and *community* in Christ's Body, the Church. The marriage of a baptized couple is a covenant between equals that celebrates their unity in Jesus Christ. They make a little family within the household of God, a "little church" in the Body of Christ.

The Protestant Reformers of the sixteenth century were unwilling to call marriage a sacrament because they did not regard matrimony as a *necessary* means of grace for salvation. Though not necessary to salvation, certainly marriage is a means of grace, thus sacramental in character. It is a covenant grounded in the reality of God's love. A Christian marriage is both a plea for and an expression of daily graces. The married couple's way of life is to be a sign of what the Church ought to be—a community of God's love. Their fidelity is a powerful indication that the Christian life is possible in our world.[4] Paul contended that marriage between a Christian and a non-Christian is also a holy union and a means for conversion (I Corinthians 7:14).

The classic purposes of Christian marriage require continuing evaluation and interpretation. These purposes, traditionally ranked, were to bear children, to avoid sin, and to enable companionship. Both the priority and the content of these purposes have been widely criticized.[5]

The view that the prime purpose of marriage is procreation is theologically and practically arguable. This purpose needs to be understood, not as a universal claim of so-called natural law, but as a decision of conscience made in marital trust and based on grace. Such a decision may or may not result in a commitment to bear children. A Christian family may complete its love with no children, through adopting or fostering children, or by planning for natural issue.

In this connection, it is significant that there has been no prayer for, or reference to, children in our marriage rite since 1792. Even the hint of children in the reference to "thy blessings upon Abraham and Sarah" has been absent since 1916.

Marriage as an expedient to avoid sin presumes a narrow view of human sexuality. It also accents a negative view of the sexual relationship. Behind these views is a long history, which contends that all sexual union is sinful, whether in the bond of marriage or not. Rather, sexual union is an expression of intimacy and love, and it is a chief means of grace and self-giving love in the marriage covenant. Sexuality is a gift of God to be accepted and enjoyed in the marriage relationship.

The third basic purpose of marriage is to establish a home, or as an old prayer book described it, "a mutual society." The Christian community of the family is more than a private friendship; it is a relationship in and of the Church as household of God. Indeed, the Roman Catholic Church in the Second Vatican Council rightly referred to the family as a "domestic church."[6] The purpose of Christian marriage, therefore, is not only to fulfill the needs of domestic intimacy, but also to enable the family to accept duties and responsibilities in the Christian community for society at large. The church witnesses to God's justice and love in both private and public life. Christian families are members of the church and citizens of the state. To paraphrase our Puritan forebears, a family is a little church and a little commonwealth; it is a school in which persons are fitted to greater matters in church and society.[7]

3. Planning the Service

Since this Service of Christian Marriage is explicitly a service of *Christian* marriage, it presupposes that one or both of the parties is Christian (see I Corinthians 7:12-14). Its Christian intention is professed by the faith of one or both of the parties and recognized by both in consenting to the union. For this reason, there will be couples for whom this service is not appropriate. It is important that clergy, in consultation with each couple, reach a responsible decision as to whether they can with integrity officiate at the contemplated wedding and as to what kind of marriage rite is appropriate.

There will also be Christian couples who prefer to be married according to another kind of marriage rite—the traditional ceremony, perhaps, or one written or adapted for the occasion. Here again, it is important that the decisions involved be responsibly made by the clergy and couple.

Those planning to use the new Service of Christian Marriage should understand that it is a celebration of the all-embracing good news of God's grace. Christian marriage is a covenant of grace undergirding the state's civil contract. Promises and claims in services for Christian marriage are something more than, and different from, the claims of the legal contract that marriage is in the eyes of the state. These Christian promises and demands go beyond the law. They are unconditional expectations of the couple, given in the public vows, exhorted in scripture and sermon, and enabled by the unswerving promises of God's unconditional mercy and love.

Christian marriage has been influenced for hundreds of years by civil prescriptions and cultural habits. In the earliest generations of the Christian era, the churches recognized civil contracts between baptized members; for several more centuries, the clergy served as literate witnesses in home weddings and later at the porch of the church.

Pre-Christian influences that linger in the wedding include the betrothal vow, giving the woman in marriage, groomsmen and bridesmaids, joining right hands, the use of rings, and signed contracts. The tradition that June is a favorite season for weddings goes back to pagan Rome and Greece. Costumes and veils, rice (a symbol of fertility), carrying the bride over the threshold, marital festivities, and honeymoons all have pagan roots.[8]

Like the celebration of Christmas, the celebration of Christian marriage can often be a delightful amalgam of profane custom and sacred rite. A purist response toward the cultural impact on Christian marriage would be unrealistic. The Christian marriage is a wedding of the earthy and the spiritual. Frequently an actual service will evidence a mixture of the solemn and the silly, pomp and sentimentality, earthiness and grace.

United Methodists pride themselves on being a nationally, racially, and culturally inclusive church. This means that local customs and ethnic traditions are desirable as well as unavoidable. The church, however, must continue to be discriminating about these influences. Marriage is an incarnational event. We celebrate a Christ who is *against* culture, *of* culture, *above* culture, *in paradoxical relationship with* culture, and *transforming* culture.[9]

The church's care for the institutions of marriage and the family is eminently pastoral. This pastoral interest in marriage is more extensive than counseling to prepare a couple for marriage, to rehearse them for the rite, to rescue them in difficulty, and to extend grace for the divorced or widowed who seek remarriage. The particular pastoral opportunities surrounding the rite of marriage are part and parcel of the church's encompassing care for families from birth to death.

Because marriage, like baptism and confirmation, is a rite of passage, people often regard the service as something the church and clergy do *to* them or *for* them. In fact, the couple marry themselves to each other in the presence of God and a company of people.

> It is the unvarying teaching of Christendom that the essence of marriage is consent. The core of all Christian marriage rites is, therefore, the point at which the two parties declare their consent to one another (and the same is true of the civil marriage rite). Thus the couple effect their own marriage by consenting to each other.[10]

The pastor is the church's official representative and witness, who presides at the service and at Holy Communion (when celebrated), announces the consent, and pronounces the blessing. The family and congregation are also witnesses and a community of faith. They affirm, give thanks, and welcome the new family within the household of faith.

The pastor enables the couple to understand both the joys and the responsibilities of marriage. The pastor also uses premarital conferences to discover the couple's story, life-style, and religious experience and commitment. Careful listening will enable the pastor to discuss practical options for the service and to witness God's grace for their married life. The concern is to celebrate both the church's faith and the participants' hope and love. The pastor has a preeminent role as Christian teacher.

Many who ask for a marriage service at the church or from an ordained minister are token believers in the Christian faith. Premarriage conferences and the rehearsal should accent the gospel and correct any impression that weddings are a theatrical ceremony. This instruction should be given to those who are being married for the first time, those who have had a civil ceremony and seek a church blessing, and the widowed and the divorced who want to be married again.

When couples come from different religious traditions, the pastor should advise them on ecumenical possibilities and courtesies. If, for example, a Roman Catholic priest will share in the service, he should be invited to take part in the premarital discussions and plans. In the service itself the clergy may share equally in the ritual. This kind of pastoral cooperation makes an important Christian witness to the families about our baptismal unity in Christ. See *An Ecumenical Service of Christian Marriage* (Fortress Press, 1987).

There is much about a marriage service that encourages congregational participation. Those who plan the service should seek involvement of all present in such acts as singing hymns, reading scriptures, responding to the vows, giving the peace, or sharing in communion.

The use of music, instrumental or vocal, expresses the joy of the event. Congregational singing is most desirable, and a choir may also sing. The music that is sung or played has great power to give the service its character, Christian or otherwise.

Because the choice of music is so important, the organist or person in charge of the music needs to be consulted in all decisions on music selection. Many local churches have adopted policies and guidelines, and musicians from outside the local church will need to be informed of them.

The organist and any other musicians involved should work together with the couple in choosing the music. Just as it is important that the integrity of the service and of the musicians be respected, so also it is important that the music speak to the needs of the couple. Since congregational participation is assumed, the tastes and repertory of the people who will be present must also be considered. Difficult decisions that stretch the usual guidelines need to be made jointly so as to protect the integrity of everyone involved. Reference recordings or actually playing or singing the music can assist the couple in selecting the music that will be appropriate for their wedding service.

The use of music written especially for the church is encouraged. It ensures the proclamation of the faith and hope of the Christian people. Such texts and music express the joy, praise, and thanksgiving that characterize marriage in a Christian context. When choosing vocal music for services of Christian marriage, one is usually on safe ground when the text is taken from the Bible or from our official hymnal.

Holy Communion may be celebrated, and the decision as to whether it is appropriate should be made by the pastor and couple. Care should be taken to avoid a "private communion" that excludes the congregation. Not only the husband and wife, but also the whole congregation are to be invited to receive communion. At the same time, communion should be administered in such a manner that there is no pressure that would embarrass those who for whatever reason choose not to receive communion.

In sum, the Christian marriage rite is a particular form of celebrating God's good news. Christian marriage, established by God in scripture, is a lifelong covenant relationship of a man and a woman. "Covenant, in contrast to contract, involves giving of self unreservedly in love to the other."[11] This union is possible when Jesus Christ is the basis and bond of unity. Christ becomes that bond of unity when the couple are centered on him. The couple encounters the risen Lord daily in their love for each other. In the community of believers, the people's witness is not just as observers. They all share in the ministry of the Word, the couple's exchange of vows, and the blessing. The Christian marriage service, whether elaborate or simple, is an act of serving God and proclaiming the lordship of Jesus Christ for the new family in the household of faith.

B. Commentary on the Order

1. The Entrance

a. Gathering

The service begins when the wedding party, family, and friends assemble at the church or other appropriate location. It is most appropriate for weddings to be held in the church where the community of the faithful regularly gathers for worship.

Instrumental or vocal music may be offered. Since the gathering time is a part of the service, the selection of music for this part, as for other parts of the service, should follow the guidelines described above. The spirit of the music should be joy, praise, and thanksgiving.

Liturgical banners and other art forms may be displayed for the gathering or used in procession. Local church policy and customs for use of candles, flowers, and other decorations should be followed. The lighting of candles before or during the gathering, or carrying them out with the going forth, can be appropriate.

A printed order of service may be provided to the worshipers by the ushers if they do not have access to copies of *The Book of Services* in the pews.

The climax of the gathering is, of course, the entrance of the wedding party. The man and woman, their witnesses, families, and other members of the wedding party enter the church or place of assembly in a manner that has been previously planned and, if necessary, rehearsed. In some congregations, it is customary for the bride and groom to stand together at the door and greet worshipers gathering before the service. The bride and groom may enter separately or together, by themselves or with members of their families. During the entrance of the wedding party, there may be instrumental music, a hymn, a psalm, a canticle, or an anthem. The following hymns, some of which are also psalms, are suggested, with their number in *The Book of Hymns:*

Come, Thou Almighty King	3
Sing Praise to God Who Reigns Above	4
Come, Ye That Love the Lord	5
Praise the Lord Who Reigns Above (Psalm 150)	15
O God, Our Help in Ages Past (Psalm 90)	28
Joyful, Joyful, We Adore Thee	38
Praise the Lord! Ye Heavens, Adore Him (Psalm 148)	42
Praise to the Lord, the Almighty (Psalms 103, 150)	55
Praise, My Soul, the King of Heaven (Psalm 103)	66
The King of Love My Shepherd Is (Psalm 23)	67
All Praise to Thee, for Thou, O King Divine	74
Jesus, Thou Joy of Loving Hearts	329
Come Down, O Love Divine	466

On the other hand, the woman and the man may enter silently and take positions visible to the assembly. The pastor(s) may join in the entrance or procession or take a position in front of the congregation to meet the wedding party.

The way in which the couple enter can be a powerful statement in itself of the relationship of the man and the woman to each other and to their families. Entering together or moving simultaneously toward each other indicates equality. To some, for the woman to come to the man seems to suggest the subordination of the woman. What is most important is that the couple and pastor realize that there are choices and make these choices responsibly.

b. Greeting

The service continues with a greeting, which welcomes the people and explains the purpose of the gathering. It may be given by the pastor or by a layperson, who may be a member of the wedding party.

While the printed text of the greeting is relatively formal, the greeting may be done informally or extemporaneously and may include introductions of the participants. If the service is being conducted informally, the congregation may exchange greetings and be explicitly invited to participate. In any event, the greeting should acknowledge that all have gathered in the sight and name of God.

Prayer may be offered before or after the greeting. If the gathering has not involved a processional hymn, a hymn of praise may be sung following the greeting.

c. Declaration of Intention

The woman and man state early in the service why they are present and give their free and mutual consent to be married. Traditionally, this declaration is equivalent to the public betrothal. It should not be confused with, or a substitute for, the actual marriage vows, which come later in the service. The declaration of intention may be omitted in the public service if desired, but the actual marriage vows are the essence of the service.

Christian marriage between a man and a woman is not a private matter. It presumes responsibility to both civil society and the Christian community. It is a legal contract freely entered into before witnesses. The couple announce in the congregation their intent to commit themselves unreservedly in the bond of marriage. They express without qualification or reservation the intention of lifelong fidelity and an acknowledgment of responsible family life.

d. Response of the Families and People

The declaration of intention calls for a response, a blessing, by the congregation. Parents or other representatives of the families, if present, may be the first to respond.

It may be the prevailing custom or personal preference that the woman's father escort her into the service and give her hand into the hand of the man. Traditionally, giving a daughter's hand in marriage was a literal gesture consummating common law agreement about dowry and property. The father of the bride gave her hand over to the groom. This handclasp transaction not only legally conveyed property, but also treated the woman as a means in the process. She was property and subordinate to the man.

These specific legal connotations and obligations have become obsolete in the service of Christian marriage. In premarital conferences, the pastor should point out that the woman is not the property of her parents to be given away and that the parents and families of both parties may wish to respond to the declaration of intention.

The text of the service provides for such a response by the parents or other representatives of the families, if they are present. This text is adaptable to a variety of family situations that may form the context of present-day weddings. The wedding couple and their families may want to offer and receive gestures of support that express their shared affection and goodwill. Whatever gestures are used here should apply equally to both the woman and the man. The verbal blessing may be accompanied by kisses, embraces, mutual handclasps, or other signs of affection and support. If either or both the man and the woman have children by previous marriage(s), it is fitting for them to join in this affirmation of support and blessing.

In any case, it is most appropriate for the congregation to express its support as provided for in the service text and perhaps also by other expressions, such as applause or the singing of a hymn, such as one of the following:

O Perfect Love	333
May the Grace of Christ Our Savior	334

e. Prayer

When the congregation and couple have gathered and been greeted in God's name, and when the couple have declared their intention and been supported by the blessing of those present, it is appropriate to praise God. In addition to the prayer printed in the text, a hymn of praise such as those mentioned above may be sung.

2. *Proclamation and Response*

It is central in public worship that the Word of God be heard by the people. This part of the service is comparable to the Proclamation and Response in the Sunday service, and while it will usually be shorter than its counterpart in the Sunday service it is nonetheless of central importance.

The various parts of this section may be led not only by the pastor(s), but also by members of the wedding party, including groom and bride, and by other family or friends.

a. Scripture and Praise

One or more scripture lessons are read. Integral to the service of Christian marriage is the proclamation of the good news of Jesus Christ. The woman and man should consult with the pastor(s) in selecting appropriate scripture readings, such as the following:

Old Testament
  Genesis 1:26-31
  Song of Solomon 2:10-13; 8:6-7
  Isaiah 43:1-7
  Isaiah 55:10-13
  Isaiah 61:10–62:3
  Isaiah 63:7-9

Epistle
  Romans 12:1-2, 9-18
  I Corinthians 12:31–13:8*a*
  I Corinthians 13
  II Corinthians 5:14-17
  Ephesians 2:4-10
  Ephesians 4:1-6

Ephesians 4:25–5:2
Philippians 2:1-12
Philippians 4:4-9
Colossians 3:12-17
I John 3:18-24
I John 4:7-16
Revelation 19:1, 5-9*a*

Gospel
Matthew 5:1-10
Matthew 7:21, 24-27
Matthew 22:35-40
Mark 2:18-22
Mark 10:42-45
John 2:1-11
John 15:9-17

Before or after readings, there may be appropriate hymns, psalms, canticles, anthem, or other music. Psalms 23, 33, 34, 37, 67, 103, 112, 145, 148, or 150 (or hymns paraphrasing them) are suggested. The accent should be on God's love and fidelity, the people's joy and thanksgiving. The organist or music director should be consulted in the selection of music.

b. Sermon or Other Witness to Christian Marriage

The purpose of a wedding sermon is to proclaim to the couple and to the congregation the Christian message of God's fidelity and what it means for the wedding and the beginning of a new life together. The sermon can proclaim the promise God gives to the union and God's act in making our union possible. Such a sermon is most effective if it is brief and to the point.

The witness to Christian marriage at this point in the service may take forms other than a sermon. One or more friends or family members may speak. The two charges at the beginning of the traditional service, or some other appropriate classical or contemporary reading, may be read as a homily. The proclamation may be choral or visual. It could be liturgical dance during readings or acts of praise.

c. Intercessory Prayer

The prayer in the service text is an intercession for the man and the woman and for their marriage. It is a prayer that their love will not only *remain* steadfast, but also continue to *grow* all their days. It may be prayed by the pastor alone, the people responding, "Amen," or it may be prayed in unison by the congregation.

As an alternative, the pastor may offer extemporaneous intercessory prayer for the couple and their marriage.

3. The Marriage

The marriage involves the public proclamation and acknowledgment of the couple's commitment. The central moment in the marriage rite occurs when the couple promise themselves to each other for life. In this marriage covenant, the couple are the principal ministers, but the pastor and congregation assist as necessary witnesses and supporters.

a. Exchange of Vows

The exchange of marriage vows by the man and the woman is their response to the gift of God's proclaimed promise, the good news of grace and love expressed in scripture. The vows printed in the text incorporate what the church understands to be the nature of the marriage covenant, which is based on the baptismal covenant. The man and the woman address each other using their Christian, or first, names.

Since this is the central act of the service of marriage, its visual and tactile impact, as well as its verbal content, is of great importance. The couple should be clearly visible to the congregation and to the pastor(s). Since the vows are spoken to each other and not to the pastor(s) or congregation, the couple should face each other and take each other by the hand when exchanging their vows.

The pastor is an official witness of the church and of the state, and the whole congregation share in the ministry of the service.

The couple marry each other in the presence of God and of the Christian community.

The phrases "as long as you both shall live" and "until we are parted by death" do not deny the reality of a reunion after death, but mean that the surviving partner is free to remarry.

b. Blessing and Exchange of Rings

We do not invoke God's blessing on inanimate objects in themselves, but on their use. If rings or other visible signs of love and mutual commitment are exchanged, it is appropriate for the minister to offer a prayer or to express the intention that these signs will be effective reminders of the couple's commitment.

The giving or exchange of tangible symbols, such as rings, is customary in the marriage rite, but it is optional. The marriage is not effected by the giving and receiving of the rings. The rings or other tangible symbols are a token and pledge of the covenant the couple has already made in their exchange of the wedding vows. This act of exchanging rings is "an outward and visible sign of an inward and spiritual grace" because the deed expresses the mutual love and trust of the couple in God and in each other. In Hispanic tradition, it is customary for the man to give the woman "arras" (coins) in addition to the ring. The spoken pledge, which accompanies the exchange, confirms that the giver is making a total and absolute commitment.

c. Declaration of Marriage

After the couple's commitment, the pastor announces, *not* pronounces, that they are now husband and wife. The pastor may place a hand on, or wrap a stole around, the couple's joined hands. In Hispanic tradition the witnesses *(padrinos)* will place the cord *(lazo)* over the husband and wife to symbolize their union.

Our society is becoming increasingly self-conscious about the significance of naming and of surnames. The scriptures have much to say about the power and identity that resides in giving and invoking names. The linking of the names of the Trinity with the names of the newly married couple is a powerful Christian witness, as it also is in Baptism. Today couples are free to choose their surnames, and whatever choice they make will both reflect and influence the character of their Christian marriage.

The congregation may respond to the declaration of marriage with an amen, a doxology, or a hymn.

Some couples may choose to have the signing of the marriage license certificate and registry at this time in the service, perhaps during the singing of a hymn.

Since the marriage takes place in the larger context of the Church and the world, intercessions may appropriately be offered at this time in the service for the Church and for the world.

d. Blessing of the Marriage

The husband and wife may stand or kneel, as the pastor offers a prayer, recalling the link between the baptismal covenant and the marriage covenant and invoking God's blessing on the woman and the man and upon their marriage. The congregation indicates by their "Amen" that they join with the pastor in this prayer.

4. Thanksgiving and Communion

If Holy Communion is not celebrated, the service continues with the Lord's Prayer and concludes with the Sending Forth.

If Holy Communion is to be celebrated, the understandings and suggestions for Holy Communion given in Part I of this book can be applied to the wedding occasion. There are, however, several matters specific to Holy Communion at weddings which should be noted.

(1) The husband and wife or representatives of the congregation may bring the bread and wine to the Lord's table.

(2) The text of the Great Thanksgiving, while following the same pattern as other texts of the Great Thanksgiving in *The Book of Services*, is designed to be appropriate to the Service of Christian Marriage.

(3) The pastor should make it clear that it is not a "private communion" of the husband and wife only but that there is an open invitation.

(4) Since there may be persons present who choose not to

receive communion, particular sensitivity should be exercised not to usher the congregation forward in such a way as to make such persons feel conspicuous or do anything else that would cause them to feel pressure or embarrassment.

5. Sending Forth

An appropriate hymn or psalm may begin the Sending Forth. While the service has been designed with the awareness that not every married couple intends to have, or can have, children, a couple may wish to include in the service something supportive of their hope for children. The use of Psalm 128 has been suggested as an option because it gives an opportunity to do this, although it presents a problem because it is addressed to the husband.

The dismissal with blessing is addressed particularly to the couple, but its blessing can be appropriated by all.

The Peace commonly begins with the kiss and embrace of the husband and wife. Those present may also exchange greetings with one another in whatever manner is customary or appropriate. If desired, the Peace may occur earlier in the service, such as before Holy Communion when it is celebrated.

As the couple, wedding party, and others present leave, a hymn may be sung or instrumental music played. This music should be triumphant and joyful. Suitable recessional hymns include "Joyful, Joyful, We Adore Thee" (38), "Now Thank We All Our God" (49), "God Is Love, His Mercy Brightens" (63), and "Love Divine, All Loves Excelling" (283).

After the service has ended, the state license, church certificate, and registry should be witnessed and signed, unless this was done during the service. In marriages involving more than one church, cross-registering is desirable.

Other courtesies, such as the greeting of guests by the wedding party and taking photographs, can be arranged in accordance with the wishes of the couple and local church guidelines.

If a reception, wedding meal, or picnic is to be held in the church or on its adjacent grounds, a joyful procession might add to the festivities.

CHAPTER V

A Service of Death and Resurrection

A. Introduction: The Ministry of the Church at Death

1. The Perspective of Christian Faith

The Christian gospel is a message of death and resurrection. The very heart of Christian faith, this message is celebrated whenever Christians worship, but it addresses the Christian community with singular power when the community must deal with human death. To repossess and restate this message is a major task of the Church in every generation. A Service of Death and Resurrection attempts to perform that task for today.

In fulfilling that purpose, the traditional funeral service is here modified and interpreted in the light of two major considerations. The first of these is the broader context of the gospel message of death and resurrection. The funeral service is treated as part of the larger process of the Christian community living out the gospel of death and resurrection, and not as an isolated rite. The Christian funeral is as much an act of corporate worship as any other worship activity, and the heart of the proclamation at a Christian funeral, as at any other Christian service, is the gospel message of death and resurrection.

The second consideration is the need to view the funeral experience within a range of interrelated perspectives: *theological* understanding, *pastoral* care, *liturgical* purpose, *psychological* knowledge, *cultural* and *ethnic* attitudes and practices, and *aesthetic* sensitivity. The variety of these perspectives makes for a fruitful tension, and openness to it should be understood, in part, as an effort to be faithful to the fourfold Wesleyan norms of scripture, tradition, experience, and reason.

More than anything else, given the primacy of scripture among these norms, Christian funeral services today need theological integrity and a clearer sense of identity as worship. Cultural pluralism and secularism have often denatured the Christian funeral of that which makes it Christian. Even Christian symbol and ritual have been corrupted by commercialization or have become dull through familiarity and habit. This discussion, therefore, begins with the context of faith and doctrine in which the funeral should be set in order for it to be Christian.

Biblical faith portrays death and resurrection in images such as Fall, Deluge, Covenant, Passover, Exodus, Promised Land, Temple, Exile, Valley of Dry Bones, Healing, and Baptism. These depict death and resurrection variously as threat and deliverance, slavery and liberation, extinction and identity, forgiveness for the past and a crossing over into a new life, brokenness and healing. The Passover-Exodus event, in particular, pervades the Old Testament and is fundamental for understanding the New Testament.

Jesus Christ in his person, his mind, his ministry, his teaching, and his saving work supremely declares the death-resurrection message. Scripture all but exhausts imagery and thought to say this. Through his conquest of death and sin, Christ as the Second Adam figures a new creation, and as Logos he incarnates the creative life of the universe. While bearing the form of God in his preexistent life, he yet humbled himself unto death and was raised as Lord that all might confess his name. In his casting out devils and healing the sick, in freeing the bound and raising the dead, the forces of life prevail over the forces of death. The truth of his teaching, which never passes away, saves from illusion and leads into eternal life. In his cross and resurrection death is destroyed, and a new heaven and a new earth have come to be. Buried and reborn with him in baptism, the Christian is nourished by his body and blood unto everlasting life. Those who trust in him as Savior, obey him as Lord, and love one another with his love have passed from death into life. In the bearing of his cross and daily denial of self, his followers find true life. In ways that the mind cannot rationally comprehend, and only faith apprehends, he comes again to judge the living and the dead. In the communion of saints, his Church, the faithful living and the faithful dead, are made one. Death and resurrection—upon this great theme the mind of the church broods in countless ways. This message is the hinge of Christian existence, the biblical verdict on the meaning and destiny of human life.

Correspondingly, this vision is the theme of Christian worship. The drama of the Christian year unfolds it. The Sunday service—a weekly Easter—and the pattern of daily prayer reenact it. Baptism as dying and rising with Christ sacramentally recapitulates it. The Lord's Supper represents it. Perhaps most directly of all, the Christian funeral proclaims it. At the most fateful moment in human experience, when the enigma of death throws us back on life's fundamental questions, the funeral liturgy declares that in the midst of life we are in death and that beyond death there is life.

In its own way, our wider human experience also echoes this theme. Life often is characterized by diminutions that in greater or lesser degree are forms of death. Jesus' insight that only as a grain of wheat falls into the ground and dies can life be brought forth rings true with many nuances of meaning. Birth itself is fraught with threat and pain. The cycles of nature unfold death and resurrection for those who have eyes to see. In our psychic history, images and myths deep in our conscious and unconscious life act out this theme, and, not surprisingly, drama and story abound with it. In our social history, the struggle against the forces of evil and death, waged in the faith that "we shall overcome" and that a better life can be won for humankind, attests to it. In our moral history, the demand to sacrifice power or privilege or possessions in order that human life may be enhanced and made more just embodies it.

Similarly, personal experience testifies that one can fully affirm life only as one truthfully affirms death. To live in reality, does not this mean accepting, not escaping, the smaller deaths—the "mortifications"—the self must daily die if a more complete life is to be had? The discipline of the scientist, the sacrifices of a parent, the asceticism of the saint—are not these diminutions accepted in hope of a richer life, which may be spoken of as a kind of resurrection? The transfiguration of suffering into meaning can sustain and nourish, even ennoble—an experience known to Christians and non-Christians alike. Does not new life in this sense depend on bearing pain that is really a partial death of the self? Is this not grief? Is not grief dying a little? And does not grief take a thousand forms? In short, grief and death mingled with new life in the funeral experience are resonant with death and life as we know them elsewhere, and the church rightly appeals to our wider experience in order better to understand its own message.

However, while biblical death and resurrection are echoed in, they are not to be equated with, our experience elsewhere, and the truth of the Church's message does not finally depend on verification by other than Christian faith. The New Testament, however its perspectives may vary in other respects, consistently underscores the reality of death and views human nature as *naturally* mortal, not immortal. Death is "enemy," not friend. Death, further, is bound up with sin. Even now, death is experienced in our lower nature that rebels against God and offends against others. The connection between death and sin cannot be set aside, if for no other reason than that people still fear death. Often this fear is deviously masked in other fears and behavioral expressions. Yet, at root, it is a metaphysical and moral fear. It is anxiety before one's ultimate destiny conditioned by the moral quality of one's life, what the Bible refers to as "unfaith" and "sin." It is in this light that the Bible makes the tremendous claim that in perfect faith and love there is no fear, that those who believe and love have already passed from death into life. Abundant evidence from the Christian experience of those who have so believed and loved validates this claim.

Similarly, Christian resurrection is not to be equated with the immortality or survival to which other areas of experience appear to bear witness. Even less is Christian resurrection to be reduced to such concepts as living on in others, reincarnation as taught in other religions, or paranormal states. For one thing, "immortality" is a negative assertion that merely claims the soul does not die. Resurrection is a positive assertion: The person is raised to life. Further, resurrection affirms life in the *body*, understood as the total matrix of personality; it does not exalt *soul* and denigrate *body* as does the concept of immortality. Also, Christian resurrection is life in community, not solitary survival of the self. Most fundamentally, Christian resurrection inheres first in God's nature, not in ours—in God's power acting to raise Jesus Christ from the dead, not in our own faculties.

Resurrection is a divine action, not a human deed. It is an act of grace, not an automatic consequence of the nature of things. As such, resurrection is both future reality and present possibility. As future, it is marked by disjunction, renewal, and reorientation of life to a quality incommensurate with what we may know or are able to imagine. This in part is the meaning of Paul's contrast of the perishable with the imperishable, the terrestrial with the celestial, and of John's assertion that while we are God's children now, it does not yet appear what we shall be. Yet, the Christian is a child of God now, and resurrection to eternal life begins, not at the moment of physical death, but of spiritual birth. Thus understood, resurrection in the light of the Christian gospel is a reality centered in Jesus Christ that ultimately is apprehended only through faith in him. It cannot be proved or disproved by empirical evidence.

However, if Christian death and resurrection cannot be defined by, or equated with, death and resurrection as encountered elsewhere, it is still true that they may be intimated by these other experiences. Death and resurrection together appear to be too deeply written into the texture of human experience to be denied. Here human truth and Christian truth, while different, yet converge. Thus, there is a certain inevitability in the theme of death and resurrection as the theme of both the funeral service itself and of the process encompassing it.

In this process and the rites that are a part of it, people will perceive the meanings of death and resurrection unevenly, on various levels, and voice these in a multitude of ways. Their perceptions as mourners may be Christian, or only theistic or humanistic or confused or secularized. Some mourners will be unable to accept or articulate the reality of death, especially if it has come as a crushing blow; to others death will be welcome as the quiet closing of a richly fulfilled life. Some people will meet death with fear and trembling as "the last enemy" to be destroyed, while to others it will seem an answer to the prayer "come, sweet death" and a joyful "going home." Indeed, the very metaphors people use or respond to will be revealing. Some will speak of death as "the great leveler," setting even the greatest of human achievements alongside the most humble. Others will regard it as the "final absurdity" in an essential absurd world. Some will conceptualize death as "sleep" or as "gate" or as "the will of God," others as "adventure" or "riddle."

Likewise, resurrection will be variously understood. To some, it will mean a fulfillment not experienced in this life, to others a ghostlike existence, to others the restoration of faculties wasted by disease, to others reunion with loved ones. To some, resurrection will mean eternal life, over which sin and death no longer have dominion, to some the vision of God, to others fire and brimstone, to others graduation onto a higher level of knowledge and understanding. Sometimes people will need to be helped toward resurrection faith; at other times faith is already so strong that it can immediately be the basis for praise and celebration.

People's understandings and misunderstandings, attitudes and reactions of whatever sort, will need both theological and psychological attention. The pastor must know the biblical faith and be sensitive to the people's needs and customs. This task requires bringing together the truth of Christian faith, the insights of psychology, a knowledge of the culture and of the subcultures in which we live, the social wisdom of custom and tradition, liturgical competence, and—informing all—pastoral compassion and care.

2. Death, Bereavement, Grief, and Mourning

To understand this task, four terms need to be distinguished that are often confusingly related to one another, but which refer to different realities. *Death* and *bereavement* denote events in people's personal history. A person dies, and others are thereby bereaved. *Grief* is the emotion caused by the event. *Mourning* is the spiritual, psychological, even moral, process of coping with and working through grief, of regaining inner wholeness and balance.

Because not all deaths are the same, *death* is experienced differently, and the nature of *bereavement* varies accordingly. The death of a person who has lived a long and useful life, who may even have looked forward to dying, is a quite different event from the untimely or tragic death of a child or youth, or of one on the verge of great usefulness. The character of the resulting *grief* and the course of the *mourning* process will consequently vary.

Experience of death also varies from one period of history and from one social milieu to another. At the beginning of this century, more than one-half of all deaths were among children. Currently, two-thirds of all deaths occur among people sixty-five years of age or older. Today, through the control of disease, the death of children in the United States averages only about 6 percent of all deaths, although among the impoverished it is much higher. While medical practice and changed social circumstances have modified the event of death and the ways we experience it, they have not altered its inevitability nor the confrontation with one's own mortality it brings to the living. The ways in which the bereaved handle this confrontation will, of course, vary. Each survivor brings to it a unique personality structure, emotional life, and religious orientation requiring pastoral sensitivity.

Whatever the nature of the death, if there are emotional ties between the deceased and the living there will be *grief.* Indeed, the degree of grief will be in proportion to the strength of these ties. In recent years, we have been able to define grief more fully and to understand its dynamics more adequately. We have learned how profound and complex an emotion it is. We have learned its many faces—tenderness, guilt, resignation, hostility, anger, peace, dependence, feelings of injustice, sometimes a new mellowness and a new breadth of understanding, and even envy of the dead when the will to live and the will to die struggle with each other. Most essentially, grief derives from love, and because love is the dynamic joining of two beings, one with the other, the merging to greater or lesser degree of self with self, pain inevitably results when part of the self is torn away. This pain—resulting from the death of oneself in another's death—is grief. Hence, grief is an honorable emotion because it is the other side of the coin of love. If we have never known love, there is little chance that we will ever know grief.

We have also learned much about grief from research in psychosomatic medicine, which investigates the reciprocal effect that emotions and the physical body exert on each other. Emotional states produce physical responses, and bodily conditions produce emotional responses. Implicit in this research is the premise that much health and illness are organic behavior, the body positively and negatively acting out its deepest feelings. Predictably, an emotion as deep as acute grief can affect virtually every body system. Thus, those who grieve should not consider themselves abnormal if they experience loss of appetite, nausea, irregularities in breathing, choking, weakness, unsteadiness, loss of muscular control, frequent crying, or dryness in the mouth or eyes. People can be helped by knowing that grief can temporarily produce quite profound changes in their bodies.

Acute grief may also manifest itself in attitudes toward God, toward other people, and toward life. Religious faith no less than other attitudes is emotionally, even physically, conditioned. Doubt, depression, even despair are not uncommon. These are usually of limited duration because the momentum of life and the will to live forged in previous experience tend to move us through them. Personal relationships may also be affected. The grieving person may become irritable, critical of others, overly sensitive to things said or unsaid, done or not done. When this happens, those who grieve should be taught to be kind to themselves and not judge themselves harshly because these feelings, too, will likely pass. However, if they do not, if a structural change of personality and attitudes persists for a substantial time, intensive counseling or psychotherapy may be called for.

The working through of grief, called *mourning*, requires a greater or lesser period of time, depending on circumstances. Estimates vary from six weeks to several months. Occasionally, the mourning necessary to restore health—physical, emotional, and spiritual—may take years. Psychologically understood, mourning is the gradual repair of the psychic wound dealt to the personality by death; the letting go of the dead part of the self and the formation, as it were, of new psychic tissue; the righting of the personality's vital balance that has temporarily been thrown into disequilibrium by destruction of part of the self.

As such, mourning must be expected to engage a person's total being. The finality of the death event needs to be inwardly appropriated and the pain of severing felt. Finitude—that is, the end of something, the ceasing to be, the awareness that the human person belongs to time and can be annihilated—must be experienced in its threat and then transcended. The self's vital energies must be removed, emotional investment in the lost object withdrawn and then redirected. Orientation toward the deceased as part of the source of the mourner's identity and dependence on the deceased as the source of the mourner's security have to be relinquished and new centers of psychic reference found. All this, of course, does not mean that the mourner ceases to love the person who has died. Rather, in emotionally letting go, the work of mourning can give back the deceased in a way that physical circumstance can never again disrupt.

However, because mourning involves dealing with the shock of finitude in an emotionally charged way, it raises anew the question of what is permanent and what is transient. It imposes the strain of stating afresh the meanings one believes are worth living for. It causes reappraisal of the values from which one had supposed one had drawn life. It compels a new decision as to where security ultimately lies. Similarly, mourning prompts the review of the survivors' past attitudes and behavior toward the deceased. Mourning exposes the poverty or the fullness with which love answered love. The sense of what religion calls sins of commission and omission is rekindled. Affirmation or rejection become understood again for what they are.

Now these are religious and moral matters, indeed even philosophical and theological ones. Hence, mourning understood as resurrection from a kind of death into a new quality of life must be comprehended in both religious and psychological ways. In particular, Christian mourning is not just self-help, and the source of new life is more than merely the process of rediscovering the self's own vitalities. Certainly these are engaged, and the processing of grieving and mourning is rightly called "work." But Christian mourning is not just "grief work," as commonly described. Rather, it is essentially an experience of divine grace. True, this grace is transmitted largely through human relationships. The beatitude, "Blessed are those who mourn, for they shall be comforted," however, locates the source of comfort in God. We do not just comfort ourselves; we are comforted. It is within this larger view that the process of death and resurrection—to which we now turn—is to be understood as enabling people to do the work of mourning and to grow in a lived experience of the gospel.

3. Steps in the Process

While the events and activities that occur after death do not follow an unfailing pattern, many steps cannot be avoided. Other steps, though optional, such as confrontation with the body of the deceased, can be suggested or encouraged. How the various steps are carried out, whether certain steps are included, and what order is followed usually depend significantly on the perceptiveness of the pastor. In order for the process to attend to both death and resurrection, the following fairly typical sequence of steps is recommended:

1. Notification
2. Confrontation
3. Ministries of the supportive community
4. The Service of Worship
5. The Committal
6. Reentry into the community
7. Continuing support of representatives of the community
8. Recurring memorial acts and services
9. Experience of congregational life

The event of death has begun the process. If death has been expected, the process may already have partially begun. The removal of an elderly person to a nursing facility, for example, sometimes long before physical death, is often experienced by both the patient and the family as the beginning of death.

a. Notification

Whether death takes place in a hospital, in a nursing home, in an accident, or elsewhere, it is usually necessary to notify others. *Notification* sets in motion a series of activities that link together all those for whom the death is significant. These include medical personnel, relatives, perhaps some of the social agencies in the community, neighbors, colleagues, and friends. As quickly as possible the pastor, the congregation, and the funeral director should be notified. The pastor should be notified immediately after the family so that the ministry of suggesting a Christian way through all the decisions that must be made can begin. Indeed, the tone of much of the process, as well as of the funeral service itself, may depend on such early notification. Of course, the pastor will not inappropriately interfere or dictate procedures that offend against expressions of caring and faith most deeply felt by the family. But if the services of a pastor are requested, the duty to help plan the funeral so that it genuinely ministers and witnesses must be discharged. This ministry begins with notification.

Usually the spontaneous reactions of those who witness or learn of death are acts—in some cases ritual acts—of mourning. The traditional covering of the face of the person who has died is one. People may spontaneously rush into each others' arms, cry together, or engage in other expressions that come naturally at such a moment. Often the pastor is present, perhaps even having brought the news. If so, the ability to perceive, to participate, to support, and to lead is of great importance. Almost certainly the pastor will offer prayer. However, initiative may rest with someone else, or people may prefer to be alone. Sometimes announcement of a death to a worshiping congregation or other assembly gives rise to spontaneous and powerful emotions that need to be acknowledged, expressed, and perhaps gathered up in prayer or song.

b. Confrontation

Confrontation of the body of the deceased is important, especially for those whose emotional involvement is great. As a kind of moment of truth, confrontation can be a crossover point when grief begins to move into mourning. Often efforts at denial so dominate emotions and thought that the palpable evidence of death is necessary to move the survivors into reality. This is true for children as well as for adults. Without confrontation with the body, the process of death and resurrection can be disabled at the outset. The bereaved may confront the body at the moment of death or shortly thereafter, when the immediate family wish to see the unprepared body, or at an arranged time for viewing after enbalming, or subsequently. In any case, it is important that the occasion and manner of confrontation not be such as to encourage tendencies toward denial. The pastor should be alert to terms and phrases such as: "going to see mother," "just the way she was," "asleep," and "slumber" because expressions like these may suggest such a tendency. A genuinely felt admission of the reality of death, insofar as a bereaved person is capable, best fosters spiritual and emotional health.

c. Ministries of the Supportive Community

The *ministries of the supportive community*—family, friends, congregation, community, pastor—are of the greatest importance. Sharing a common sense of loss, the community surrounds the grief-stricken with their physical and spiritual presence. Calling at the house or funeral home, bringing in food, giving assurances of prayer, bringing or sending flowers, sending written messages, and assisting with arrangements are typical forms of ministry. Even when those ministering think they have found nothing to say, each word and gesture bears a certain grace. Because such ministries are exceptions to the routines of life, they mark the intrusion of death and, as such, reinforce its reality. Because they are emotional expressions, they give resonance to grief and provide the climate in which strong feelings can be poured out and healing begins to take place.

Further, when intentionally understood as *ministries*, they also mark the members of a congregation as *church*. The pastor-hood—as well as the priesthood—of believers is made tangible. The Christian graces of faith, hope, and love are visibly acted out. Because the shock of death of one member affects all, the entire congregation can become reengaged with the meanings of death and resurrection. They are turned back on themselves and on their faith. They are recalled as a Christian community to their foundations, made to reexamine their life in Christ, to repent, to renew their faith, and to rededicate themselves to service in Christ's name.

d. The Service of Worship

The service of worship, commonly spoken of as the funeral, brings to focus the larger process of death and resurrection. Most of the discussion of this service is reserved for the commentary on the service that follows, but there are a few fundamental considerations that call for discussion here.

(1) The service is an act of Christian worship. If it is considered necessary to alter its distinctively Christian character, the service should then not be entitled "A Service of Death and Resurrection." Even though the connection between death and resurrection as defined in biblical faith and as known in common experience be retained, if Christian meanings are not kept sovereign, then the integrity of the service is lost. Fundamental to any Christian funeral service is the proclamation of Jesus Christ as Savior from death and sin and as Lord of life. Here, as elsewhere in Christian worship, Christ holds the service. Christ is host; the worshipers are guests. The words and actions of pastor and people are human means through which Christ can save, heal, and raise to newness of life; to this healing and salvation, the people respond in the offering of themselves. Thus to name a non-Christian service with a Christian name would be false for all concerned. The pastor should have in mind such essentials as these and realize what is being done if they are ignored.

(2) The Service of Death and Resurrection is both comforting and confrontational. Or, to speak more accurately, it truly comforts only when it also confronts. Failure to grasp this biblical truth accounts for much of the corruption in funeral services today. At stake here is reality—the people's and pastor's sense of reality and the honesty of their intention to be led into reality. Also at stake is the question of what true comfort is. Christian death and resurrection hold implications for faith and morals that cannot be evaded even at such a poignant moment as death. Only as these meanings are made clear will the service deal honestly with what is vital to the people. Otherwise, the existential questions death raises will not be faced; the people will not be ministered to on the deepest levels of their being; and comfort will only be something experienced as emotionally transient on the surface level. Here lies the danger of conceiving the funeral only

psychologically and therapeutically. *The Spirit that comforts is the Spirit of truth,* as the fourteenth and sixteenth chapters of John's Gospel make abundantly clear; the truth into which the Spirit leads is the evangelical truth of a merciful and moral God, the truth of faith and love, and the truth about ourselves and about life. Not surprisingly, really to be confronted with these meanings does usually become, in one way or another, death and resurrection.

(3) The Christian funeral is by definition corporate. It is an action by a called community that gathers believers as well as all who grieve to whatever degree. Every person is potentially both a mourner and a comforter of others, and all are to do the work of worship together. This corporate character is both visible and invisible. It includes both those physically present and those of all times and places who are gathered in Christ, the communion of saints on earth and in heaven. Consciousness of the communion of saints does not imply, of course, that the reality of death is denied. It does require that the phrase "the living" be given scriptural force and point.

(4) It flows from this understanding of the service that whenever possible the funeral should be conducted in the congregation's regular place of assembly. This very setting reinforces perception of the service as an act of worship. Even when the deceased or family are unconnected with the church, it should not be assumed that a church service is not desired. The act of contacting a minister may itself indicate a reaching out for the ministry and fellowship of the church. The very existence of a church building is a witness to the gospel. Consecrated and dedicated for just such occasions of worship as the Service of Death and Resurrection, it is unusually rich in symbols of faith; it evokes memory and association; it is infused with the experience of the worshiping community. It offers a place designed and furnished for worship—with the pulpit and pulpit Bible, the Lord's table and facilities for Holy Communion, the baptismal font that reinforces the tie between the funeral and baptism, organ, hymnals, service books, and a total visual environment conducive to worship. Neither the coffin nor flowers should visually obscure the Lord's table and central symbols of faith, such as the cross. If the service is held in a funeral home, everything

possible should be done to make the setting proper for Christian worship and to provide symbols of church and faith, such as cross, pulpit Bible, vestments, hymnals, and candles. Above all, the appointments and arrangements should insure that the coffin is not the center of worship.

(5) The gospel, it must be remembered, is experienced and communicated in much more than words. Architecture, stained glass, and the appointments of the church proclaim meaning. Lighted candles also speak of life in the midst of death, summon the believer to watchfulness, and announce the presence of One who is the Light of the world. Flowers symbolize life in the midst of death. Vestments, altar cloths, banners, and any special clothing worn by mourners speak of both grief and faith. A cloth pall, designed with Christian symbolism and used to cover the coffin during the service, witnesses to the new life "put on" in Christ. At funerals in some cultures, masks are used. In many Christian traditions, Holy Communion, which engages all our senses, is regularly celebrated.

(6) Music variously combines strains of grief and victory. In certain congregations in New Orleans, for example, a marching band plays somber music on the way from the church to the cemetery and exultant jazz music on the return home. Even the way in which pallbearers carry the coffin, the manner in which mourners greet one another, the way in which the pastor welcomes the family to church or funeral home, the bodily movements of people and pastor in processions, the physical conduct of and participation in the service—all such ceremonies and symbols can witness to Christian meanings.

(7) As a corporate act, the service ministers to the congregation and friends as well as to the family. The pastor acts as the representative of the congregation and of the universal Church. The pastor's personal relationship with the deceased and the family is very important, but pastoral responsibility transcends these relationships. On occasion, for example, a family may request a private service. While sensitive to their feelings, the pastor should strongly discourage this practice. It diminishes the congregational character of worship. It excludes others who by their presence could contribute support to the family. It can close off emotions that need to be expressed. A grief shared is a grief

reduced; a grief withheld is a grief amplified. In particular, a private service can deprive mourners of the objective witness of others' faith, which can help set the pain felt at death within the promise of experienced renewal.

(8) The corporate nature of the funeral also requires that the congregation participate fully in the service—singing together, weeping together, praying together, affirming faith together. There is no reason why the laity cannot conduct much of the service. The family, also, should be part of the congregation and not isolated from them, and their participation in conducting parts of the service should also be encouraged. Worship, at the funeral service as elsewhere, belongs to all the people, not to the pastor or the funeral director, or even to the grieving family. Even when no mourners attend and only the pastor and mortuary staff are present, the pastor still represents the church local and universal, visible and invisible; who can say what pastoral ministry may or may not mean even to the funeral home staff itself at such a time?

e. The Committal

The *committal* is usually the next step in the process. It is important, however, to observe here that the concept of committal has several meanings. (1) There is the committal of the body to the earth—or, in the case of cremation, to the elements. (2) There is the committal of the deceased person to God. (3) There is the committal, or recommittal, of the people themselves to God. The latter two are sometimes referred to liturgically as "commendation" or "offering." These three meanings are interrelated, and provision for all of them is evident in the Service of Death and Resurrection.

(1) Committal, in the first meaning of the term, may take place immediately following the Service of Worship or at a later time, depending in part on the place of burial, the distance the body must be transported, cemetery regulations as to when burials may take place, and the season of the year. Committal of the body can also take place immediately after death and be followed as soon as possible by a service of worship, in the church or elsewhere. When a number of days intervene between the private committal and the later public service, the mourners may have difficulty bringing

closure to this stage of the mourning process. In any case, the committal service should whenever possible be conducted at the burial site. Only when conditions make this unfeasible should it be held in the church, funeral home, or cemetery chapel. Committal of the body or its ashes may be by earth burial, by entombment above ground, by burial at sea, or (in the case of ashes) by scattering.

Whatever form it takes, the committal is to be understood and conducted as an act of worship. For the Christian, the body has been the temple of the Spirit of God. It has been valued and loved. When it no longer serves its purposes in its old form, it is returned to the elements from which it came with thanksgiving to God for the gift of its wonder. Here the mourners, brought face to face with the finitude of physical life, are thrust back to spiritual realities. For this reason, among others, it is desirable that the family be present and participate in this action.

(2) The committal of the deceased person to God is, of course, implicit throughout the entire process of death and resurrection. Psychologically, many mourners may most poignantly associate it with committal of the remains. Religiously, it comes to fullest expression in various parts of the Service of Death and Resurrection, notably those that call the deceased by name (using the Christian or baptismal first name) and in intercessory prayer for the dead.

There are strong reasons—theological, historical, liturgical, and psychological—in favor of prayer for the dead. Protestant aversion to the Roman Catholic doctrine of purgatory and reaction against abuses of the mass for the dead have too often become unthinking overreaction and should no longer blind us to the fact that prayer for the dead has been a widespread practice throughout Christian history. It probably derived from Judaism and was an integral part of the Eucharist, which was celebrated in connection with the Christian funeral at least as early as the third century.

Theologically, prayer with the dead is inherent in all Christian worship. Because Christian worship is corporate by definition, the prayer of the church on earth is joined with that of "all the company of heaven" who praise and magnify God's holy name. But Christian prayer is not merely prayer *with*, but it is also prayer *for*, the dead. As such, it is a profound expression of faith. It is a way of affirming the reality of shared life in Christ's body, a body not subject to temporal and spatial bounds.

Even more, prayer for the dead is a profound act of love addressed to a God of love. The instinct to pray to God for those whom we love and to desire their good is surely as valid for the dead as for the living. Love, we are rightly told, *"never* fails"; if love as prayer has been offered for people up until the moment of death, we can hardly expect survivors to cease offering love as prayer after death. Above all, *God's* love does not cease being the same love after death that it was before, and its very nature is that it is vulnerable to human importunity. Indeed, it is a love whose expression seems to need the human agency of prayer. It is a love, also, that, undeterred by the ignorance of our petitions, translates their meaning in terms of the love behind them. Thus, if one doubts the truth of intercessory prayer for the dead, it would be well to rethink one's understanding of God, one's Christology, and one's doctrine of the church.

Now this does not mean, of course, that such prayer is to be foisted on resistant people, but it does mean that the question of prayer for the dead is a very important one. The pastor may need to reflect on this issue with the congregation as part of their pastoral education without relation to a specific death in their midst.

(3) Committal also takes the form of the offering and reoffering by the people of themselves to God. Liturgically, the offering of the person who has died can be an act through which the people also offer their "very selves," souls and bodies, a living sacrifice holy and acceptable to God, their spiritual service. Thus understood, what is called "The Commendation" in the service becomes the climax of the process of death and resurrection and recapitulates the core reality of Christian faith and experience. Psychologically, also, this action is of immense importance. The self in all its brokenness—faith mingled with doubt, love with perhaps bitterness and fear—can be unified in God. Spiritually, the very anguish of offering oneself despite these tangled feelings can be a meeting with Christ's judgment and mercy, a dying to one's former life, and being raised to a new life. Ethically, committal in this sense can recenter and redirect the self by

placing on it that yoke of love for others by which the self knows that it has passed from death to life. In short, the offering of self within the contemplation of death acts to illumine the meaning and destiny of life.

Here lies in part the rationale for celebrating Holy Communion in the funeral service. While communion holds many meanings that relate to death and resurrection—thanksgiving, repentance and confession, memorial, anticipation—its heart is the encounter with the crucified and risen Christ, who offers himself to us, and the offering of our lives to Christ.

f. Reentry into Community

Reentry into community is usually marked by such actions as the family's last gathering and dispersing, the homely tasks of acknowledging kindnesses and caring for business affairs, the resumption of work, and return to the worship and activities of the congregation. One custom in this part of the process calls for special comment—the bringing and sharing of food at what is often a post-service common meal. Practical needs are met by this custom, and it also exercises much spiritual power. Meals have profound meaning in Christian experience and tradition; it was "in the breaking of bread" that Christ made himself known. The common meal, either at home or at church after the committal service, can function as a parallel to Holy Communion. Indeed, the sequence of (1) service of the Word, (2) committal, and (3) common meal may be experienced as a unity not unlike the classical pattern of Word and Table. Sensitively understood, this meal can be a means of grace and a source of renewed life. It can do much to restore the mourners to the community around them and symbolize the ongoing nurture that people offer to one another.

g. Continuing Support of Representatives of the Community

The long-range *continuing support* the mourners receive *from representatives of the congregation and community* is vital. In the first days after death has occurred, people may have come in large numbers to offer support, but the time of greatest need usually comes in the weeks following. Then the state of numbing shock has worn off and the sharp reality of loss is experienced. Then the days are no longer crowded with duties and decisions, and there is time to reflect. Then friends and relatives are less likely to be present to comfort.

The pastor's ministry here is vital, but laypeople able and willing to enter into a long-range relationship can also be trained to minister at this time and represent to the mourners the larger community. Those who have known grief can be trained to help others deal with grief in its many forms. Questions of faith, of values, and of life purpose can be faced together. The ministry of the laity and the priesthood of believers can be made real.

Particularly important are the pastor's first calls on the family after the service and the committal of the body have taken place. The pastor's symbolic and functional roles and the people's perception of the pastor—as symbol of the gospel and of the church, as friend, as counselor, perhaps as priest—should be rethought here. In these calls, the family can be helped to make the transition from initial grief to the long-range work of mourning that lies ahead. The part the pastor may play can be discussed and clarified. Symptoms of normal and abnormal grief can be identified. Estimates can be made of the help that may be necessary in the form of prayer, counseling, healing and reconciliation ministries, and the administration of Holy Communion. The grieving may also be invited to join, or even to help form, a long-term spiritual support group with others of similar needs.

In this part of the process, of course, situations will vary. It must be expected that some people will find more difficulty in experiencing mourning as death and resurrection than others. Some will be better prepared emotionally and spiritually, others less well. Where senility of the deceased or other conditions before death have already caused the relationship with the survivors to be partially or wholly severed, mourning may already be well advanced. Shock will disable others, or personality structures may inhibit or contort. Religious faith may be neurotically or healthily used. The costs of growth in faith and health may be refused and merely temporary adjustment mistaken for resurrection. The pastor must be aware of such possibilities.

h. Recurring Memorial Acts and Services

From time to time, the mourning process will come to sharper consciousness in *recurring memorial acts and services*. The memory of the deceased will be especially poignant on occasions such as Christmas, holidays, birthdays, and the anniversary of the death. This will also be the case on occasions of other deaths or when anything else happens that particularly reminds people of death and of those who have died. On such occasions, the mourner is particularly open to supportive ministries, such as a visit, placing memorial flowers on the grave or in the church, sending handwritten notes of remembrance and sympathy, or naming the dead in the church bulletin or service or prayer. Many congregations annually observe the festival of All Saints—on November 1 or on the first Sunday in November—or some other memorial Sunday when the communion of saints is celebrated and those who have died within the year are named. The celebration of Holy Communion is particularly appropriate on such an occasion. At weekly Sunday services, and especially when Holy Communion is celebrated, the dead may likewise be remembered in prayer. Through such pastoral and liturgical ministries, the meaning of death and resurrection is relived; death is faced and life is reaffirmed.

i. Experience of Congregational Life

In a broader sense, the mourners' *experience of congregational life* in its totality—through its educational program, its evangelism, its mission, and its worship—also conditions the process of death and resurrection. Because the message of death and resurrection is central in scripture and in the Church's faith, it should inform the total life of the congregation. The way people deal with death when it comes will depend on how forceful the impact of this message has been on their consciousness through the structures of congregational life.

Death and life after death are commonly perceived in our culture today, for example, in secular and pseudoscientific terms, and laypeople's attitudes are more often shaped by newspaper journalism, magazines, films, and best-selling books than by

Christian teaching. Changing attitudes toward death and the supernatural are certainly to be learned from, and the varied meanings of death and resurrection are to be identified in our experience generally. The discerning pastor, however, will take care that a congregation's educational program helps people to know the Christian meaning of these realities and to distinguish truth from fad, faith from superstition, and Christian teaching from occult speculation.

Similarly, congregational evangelism needs to be scrutinized in the light of the death-resurrection message. Evangelism in some congregations today appears to result in a programmed experience of easy grace, rather than a costly dying and rising with Christ. But only as the fatefulness of a decision for Christ is brought home to people in a congregation's evangelistic outreach can they deal as Christians with fate, death, and the other crucial points in their existence.

Mission, likewise, requires a congregation to be aware of the forces of death and evil in society—such as oppression, militarism, racism, sexism, materialism, hedonism, greed, and corruption—and to affirm life over against them. Truly, death and the diabolic bear many faces; physical death is only one of them. Likewise, resurrection as God's calling into being of not-yet-existent life takes many forms, and in a profound sense the mission of a congregation is precisely to be agents of resurrection amid forces of social death. To pass from death into life is not an experience reserved until people die physically. Christians can know this experience now.

Probably the ongoing worship life of a congregation most powerfully determines people's perception of death and resurrection at the funeral as well as in the process that encompasses it. Insofar as preaching, the Lord's Supper, baptism, confirmation, and other renewals of the baptismal covenant have been structured by this central message, it will be real; insofar as they have not, it will not be real. Indeed, only as the total spectrum of congregational worship is formed by the theme of death and resurrection can it vitally form people in Christian faith. This is why the frame of the Christian year is so crucial. Its very pivot is the Christian Passover of Holy Thursday/Good Friday/Easter. Its seasons and festivals are but variations on this theme, and in its totality it is the drama of Christian reality within which all else unfolds. Thus a kind of judgment on a congregation's worship life is pronounced at its funerals. Whether people come to times of bereavement poorly or well prepared says much about the integrity of congregational worship as the people have experienced it.

4. Memorial Services

Many persons have requested resources for *memorial services* and for use in the event that the body is cremated or donated for medical purposes. The name *memorial service* denotes a service at which the body is not present, as distinct from a funeral, where the coffin containing the body is present. Often the question is raised whether memorial services are fundamentally different from funerals and call for a different order of worship with a different rationale.

In dealing with this issue, it is important to emphasize that every funeral in one sense is a memorial service. Further, it is important to distinguish several types of services frequently called memorial services.

(1) There are annual memorial services *commemorating the dead,* such as those mentioned above. Many congregations hold such services, as do many secular groups, such as veterans' organizations. These are highly appropriate as part of the process of experiencing death and resurrection, as preparation for the death of participants, and as a continuation of the work of mourning for those who grieve.

(2) Memorial services are also held *on the anniversary of the birth or death* of prominent historical figures, such as Martin Luther King, Jr. Jewish Yahrzeit rites on the anniversary of the death of a member of one's family are an example from another religious tradition.

(3) Sometimes memorial services are held *in addition to a funeral service* for the benefit of those unable to attend the funeral. A group of mourners may live too far from the scene of the funeral to attend. The time or the season of the year may not be convenient. Those who wish to attend may be hospitalized or otherwise

incapacitated, and a simple memorial service in the hospital or home may be appropriate. When a well-known person dies, the family may wish a less public funeral followed by a larger memorial service.

(4) A memorial service is sometimes held *in place of a funeral.* Probably this is the type of service most commonly referred to when the question of memorial services is raised. Such a service is sometimes held because the body of the deceased has been destroyed or cannot be recovered or for some other reason is unavailable. The body may have been donated for medical purposes or buried without public ceremony by family decision or out of respect for the expressed wishes of the person who has died.

Cremation, the reduction of the body to bone fragments by use of intense heat, can be practiced in connection with either a funeral or a memorial service. Sometimes the body is cremated without the mourners' having the opportunity to confront it, sometimes following such a confrontation but before a public service, and sometimes following the public service. The ashes may be buried in the ground, placed in a vault above ground, or scattered.

Such a variety of possibilities makes clear the wisdom of being cautious in making blanket generalizations about memorial services. A few general observations, however, can be made.

Most orders of service for funeral or burial, including the Service of Death and Resurrection, can readily be adapted for a memorial service and for use in cases of cremation or body donation. Indeed, a memorial service should generally contain as far as possible the same elements as a funeral. The committal of the body will, of course, be eliminated. If the pastor has been asked to serve in the office of Christian minister and the family and mourners consider the occasion to be Christian worship, the Christian gospel should certainly be proclaimed at a memorial service as at other services of the church. Perhaps the service may focus more directly on the life of the deceased than would be the case at a funeral, but this change should not be difficult, and the integrity of the service as Christian worship need not be impaired. In fact, the Service of Death and Resurrection provides for this change in the optional acts of "naming" and "witness" more aptly than traditional funeral services have done. The choice of prayers and scripture readings provided in the service takes into account a wide range of situations. The freedom to select music and to adapt the service itself as needed give the pastor and family the ability to deal with an even wider range of circumstances.

Nevertheless, the service with the body present is to be preferred. This practice is in accord with Christian tradition and its respect for the body as part of human and Christian being. It also accords with the love deep in our nature that desires to affirm the person of the deceased by honoring the body. It is not an exaggeration to say that the presence of the body marks the incarnational nature of human love, and a service without such a visible reminder in a sense denatures love of that which most poignantly conveys its reality. The presence of the body can also protect against the tendency to spiritualize death away and to gloss over its starkness. New Testament faith does not shrink from such confrontation—death is death. Further, such confrontation therapeutically contributes to making the mourning process less difficult. For the living, resurrection depends on internalizing the reality of death. Only as this internalization is painfully lived through and appropriated can full healing usually take place. Psychiatric evidence of the ill effects when internalization does not take place underscores this point.

At services where the body is not present, it is important to do what is possible to facilitate the confrontation with, and realization of, death. The language used should not evade reality. Visible reminders, such as pictures or other tokens of the person who has died, can also help. It may be possible to provide the opportunity prior to the services for those who wish to see the body to do so, especially the immediate family. At the final disposition of the remains, by whatever method, care should be taken straightforwardly to name death as death and body as body.

5. For Those Outside the Church

Another question frequently arises: What kind of service should be held for *non-Christians or the unchurched?* Frequently, services are requested for people who have formally belonged to the Christian community, but have given no evidence of Christian commitment, who have not been church members, though they have considered themselves Christian, who have professed a religion other than Christianity, or who have professed no religion at all. Furthermore, whatever the religious commitment of the deceased, there may be the widest differences of faith and commitment among the mourners. The suggestion has been made that a special service, or services, be provided for such occasions.

After careful consideration, it was decided not to provide such a separate service for *The Book of Services.* The choice of prayers and scriptures provided in the Service of Death and Resurrection makes it adaptable to a wide variety of situations. The pastor is free to minister as may be judged appropriate according to circumstances. Certainly it is important always to be circumspect in indicating how any person stands before God. Further, and common to all people—Christian or non-Christian, churched or unchurched—is the basic respect for every human life and, correspondingly, the wish to provide a decent burial. Surely the pastor's duty and desire will be to honor this respect. The Service of Death and Resurrection is not to be an occasion for rejection or manipulation, but for genuine care and outreach.

The Service of Death and Resurrection is intended to be a proclamation of the gospel, but there should be no conflict between this affirmation and the requirements of sensitive pastoral care. There is every reason to assume that when people request the services of a Christian pastor, whatever their religious commitment, they expect the pastor to minister as a Christian; surely the pastor's own conduct and sensitivity can be a Christian witness. The gospel here may be better acted than spoken, but it can also be spoken in ways that respect the integrity of the hearers. The pastor's witness need be no less a proclamation of the gospel if, out of respect for others, the service is not held in the church building or is not called a Service of Death and Resurrection or omits certain words or acts of worship that might give offense. If circumstances call for sharing leadership of a service with someone of a different religious commitment, surely each can witness with integrity while respecting the faith of the other.

Indeed, there is probably ambivalence in all who mourn, which should be faced openly in the perspective of the gospel. Each of us brings to death and grief a mixture of doubt and faith, of fear and confidence, of that which makes for death and that which makes for life. It is precisely in the light and strength of the gospel that we can look honestly at all this, be humbled before truth, enter more fully into reality about ourselves and God, and find help in time of need.

In this vein, we also address what must be for some pastors the hardest question: How can I help others and give them the assurance they need if my own faith is faltering? One may find an answer in Paul's insight that we are "stewards of the mysteries of God" (I Corinthians 4:1). We are servants and agents of a grace whose efficacy does not depend on our own faith or virtue. As stewards do not possess what is entrusted to them, so pastors who read the great passages of scripture, pray the prayers of the Church, preach gospel they themselves do not entirely under-stand, and allow Christian symbols to be seen and music of faith heard are letting God make them instruments of a gospel greater than the feeble faith any of us can bring. The pastor can surely receive as well as give at the Service of Death and Resurrection.

6. The Ministries of Others

The officiating minister should be sensitive to the ministries performed by others. Many are called upon to minister at the time of death, and the pastor's ability or inability to work with them can greatly help or hinder the effectiveness of these ministries.

For the benefit of all concerned, the pastor should have a sound working relationship with the funeral directors of the community. In hardly any other public capacity does the pastor work so closely with another care-giving profession. Rivalry or misunderstand-ings can disserve the bereaved and interfere with a properly conducted funeral. It is wise, as early as possible in a pastorate, for the pastor to make friends with the funeral directors in the community and discuss with them how they can best cooperate. The pastor's perception and policies as to the nature of the funeral and its proper conduct should be made clear, as should the perceptions and policies of the funeral director. Differences and disagreements should be worked out in a spirit of mutual understanding and respect.

Good relationships between the pastor and the church or funeral home musician are also important. It is vital that the musician respect the pastor's role and authority as the leader of worship and as the one having a unique relationship with the mourners. It is also vital that the pastor respect the musician's standards and musical integrity. Both should discuss in advance their views on such questions as the qualities that make music suitable for worship at a funeral and the place in funerals of congregational singing, of solos, of live instrumental music, and of recorded music. How does one determine, for example, when a solo is a helpful witness, a true act of worship, an artistic display, or a too-easy substitute for congregational participation? Prior to a service, the pastor should be consulted by musician and family regarding the purpose and place of music in the service. Rather than attempting to serve as intermediary between family and musician, however, the wise pastor will refer the family to the musician.

Similarly, the pastor needs to understand the ways in which friends and family minister to one another. Customs and practices that may at first sight seem strange often have in them much wisdom when the total context is known. There are rich varieties of ethnic practices, many regional folk customs, and wide diversity in the traditions of particular families and in individual expectations. These are not without fault, of course, but given the background out of which they come they often make excellent sense. Two people may be mourning with equal honesty; one may cry profusely, even scream, while the other weeps inconspicuously and silently. Music that comforts some people will seem inappropriate to others. Some people perceive distinctive styles of clothing as appropriate for funerals, while to others the question does not matter. An elaborate floral display, a single rosebud, or a donation to a significant cause may each be, from their respective donors, the most eloquent of gifts. A magnificent coffin that some people would consider a terrible waste of money, a simple coffin that others might consider stingy, a pall covering a coffin of whatever sort, may each, in context, be true expressions of faith and caring. The value of a funeral is determined not by its financial cost or by its conformity to a particular custom, but by the effectiveness of its Christian witness and of its ministry to people.

Understanding and sensitivity are especially needed between people of different generations. Mourners at the death of persons in their teens or twenties, for instance, will include parents and others of the parents' and grandparents' generations as well as friends of the deceased and, perhaps, brothers and sisters and their spouses of more or less the same age. What seems loving and appropriate to one group of mourners may not seem so to another. When the untimeliness of a death and perhaps its violent nature as well—by accident, suicide, or as a result of crime or war—have caused grief to be exceptionally intense, one group of mourners may especially need to be made more sensitive to the emotions and needs of another.

7. Children and Death

It is also important to be sensitive to the effect of death on children. A child can have a vital, full emotional life and religious faith, although framed by limited experience. Children can know acute grief even though they do not understand the meaning of death. They, too, need opportunity for ceremonial acting out in order to grow in faith and to deal with their feelings. Sometimes adults—perhaps projecting their own anxieties—determine that children should not attend a funeral. Studies have shown, however, that children are more likely to be emotionally injured by being denied the opportunity to confront the body of a dead person and to experience a funeral service than by being allowed to participate at their own level of understanding. Just as a flower girl does not need to understand all about marriage and human sexuality in order to perform her role at a wedding, so also a child does not need to understand all about death in order to participate in a funeral.

We need always to remember that children are threatened by deceit. Not only does deceit deny them the answers they require for healthful growth in understanding, but it also undermines confidence in those to whom they look for understanding. Children have built-in sensitivities to lies. They perceive when they have been denied the truth, and distrust may impel them to use their imaginations in damaging ways. While it is unwise to force a child to attend a funeral, a child's refusal to share in such an important family activity may signal that already a child is responding to anxiety in a damaging way. Children need direct, honest, and simple answers to their questions. Either to deny an answer or to over-answer is to foster anxiety in a child's life.

Adults should also be aware of the developmental process and of the stages of a child's capacity for awareness and for perception and should respond to children's needs according to their level. Children have long lives ahead of them, and it is extremely important that they be guided into healthful attitudes toward death and into honest faith. Mishandled anxiety in the face of death—and the unhealthy fantasy it fosters—has been shown to be one cause of nonrational behavior, indulging in drugs, and playing life-threatening games. A realistic confrontation, which includes even a certain fear of death, on the other hand, when set within supportive relationships and religious faith, can stabilize behavior and enable a child to cope with other fears that life inevitably brings. From the funeral experience, children can learn that their own life is valued and valuable and that it is in the hands of a loving God.

B. Commentary on the Service

1. The Entrance

a. Gathering

A Service of Death and Resurrection, like any order of Christian worship, should provide for proclaiming the gospel in a way that authentically ministers to people. This proclamation is initiated in the entrance rite and even as the people gather.

Proclaiming (from *clamo*, meaning "call" or "cry aloud") is first of all, however, an action of God that precedes, although it also takes form in, the people's action. Gathering is thus the people's acting out the nature of Christian assembly as both divine convocation (from *con vocare*, meaning "to call together") and human congregation (from *con grex*, meaning "together" or "flock"). It is the people's defining themselves as "the called"—that is, as the *ecclesia* (from the Greek *ek kaleo*, meaning "call out")—as church. The first emphasis, however, is on God and on the priority of God's grace in calling and recalling through Jesus Christ. In bodily movement, gesture, music, spoken words, and symbols, pastor and people simultaneously express and are impressed with this meaning.

Assembly at the Christian *funeral*, however, is distinctive because the realities proclaimed in all true Christian worship— mercy, judgment, and resurrection to new life—are proclaimed here literally in the face of death. Hence the funeral, as distinguished from other gatherings of the Church, embodies an intensity of confrontation with death and resurrection that marks it as unique. This does not mean that either the gathering or the funeral is to be threatening or predominantly penitential, nor is the seriousness of the occasion to be equated with somberness. Joy contrapuntally mingles with sorrow. What the confrontation *does* mean is that the funeral is in part a converting and a reconverting ordinance; hence, the gathering begins both a salvational and a healing event. In this sense the funeral is a liturgical microcosm of the arresting truth: "You [God] made alive while you were dead in trespasses and sins" (see Ephesians 2:1-10).

The people will perceive this meaning unevenly. It may become real only as the service progresses or at a later time, or it may not become real at all. Yet, the funeral can truthfully be an "Easter liturgy," as it is often described, only if it is also in some sense a "Good Friday liturgy." In Christian experience, the "Hallelujah Chorus" and the "Lord, Have Mercy" go together. The gathering initiates this realization.

While the pastor presides at the funeral, the service is not the pastor's but the church's and the people's. This is the truth underlying the principles of corporateness and participation, noted previously. The liturgical requirement in the gathering is not only that the people become physically present, but also, even more, that they act to manifest their presence to one another before God so that a communion is established in which they can do the work of worship together. Throughout the service, beginning with the gathering, the people should be fully involved, although naturally and without manipulation. This is one reason that the order of service should be available for use by the congregation.

Too often the gravity of the funeral service becomes a disabling stiffness. A certain solemnity is almost inevitable, but there is no reason why pastor, friends, and members of the congregation should not welcome the family and other mourners to the place of the service in a natural way. Perhaps in a room other than the sanctuary or chapel, greetings may be exchanged, prayer offered, music sung, food shared, letters and messages read, and pictures and objects associated with the deceased displayed and talked about. Local custom will no doubt affect decisions here; and the human character of the congregation should find natural, unaffected expression. This human touch may occur in other parts of the service or at an occasion after the service.

In the sanctuary or chapel itself, the people are not only gathering physically but "getting it all together" spiritually as well, and the environment should be conducive to this. Before or during the gathering, candles in the chancel may be lit. The coffin, whether it is already in place or outside and about to be brought in, may be covered with a pall. Instrumental or vocal music for worship may be offered while the people gather. When enough people have gathered, they may wish to sing hymns and songs of faith.

Generally it is desirable to cover the coffin with a pall. Palls, or patterns from which church members can make a pall, are readily available from church supply houses, or members of a congregation may design and make their own. The same pall is used in a congregation for all funerals; this makes all coffins, however plain or extravagant, equal before the table of the Lord. A pall not only denotes the community and democracy of all members, but also it connects the service with the new life a Christian puts on at baptism and prefigures the purification that faith looks forward to in Christ. It is important that the pall be clean and free of wrinkles for each funeral. Flowers are never placed on top of the pall. The family or friends of the deceased may place the pall over the coffin.

As they do so, the pastor may say the words given in the text, which proclaim the basis of the Service of Death and

Resurrection in the baptismal covenant. They set the human life of the deceased within the divine life of Christ, first "put on" as a child of God at baptism. At the same time, they quietly affirm in the words of I John 3:2-3 the promise of life with Christ after death for all people of faith. So important are these words in expressing the meaning of the service that, if a pall is *not* placed on the coffin during the gathering, these words should still be used somewhere early in the service, such as following the word of grace and greeting.

The liturgical color used in the service for the pall, in the pastor's stole, and in the chancel paraments should signify the meanings of the gospel of death and resurrection. While a variety of colors can be used, the basic, or background, color of most recently made palls is white. White signifies both death and resurrection. On the one hand, white is widely used as a color of mourning in many African and Asian cultures. Even in Western cultures an association of the color white with death is shown, for instance, in the phrase "white as a ghost." On the other hand, white has predominantly been used in Christian tradition and practice to symbolize resurrection, new life, purity, joy, and celebration. On the white background can be a cross, a crown, a sheaf of wheat, vines or branches with leaves, and other appropriate symbols. Appropriate colors for these include gold, signifying joy and celebration, and green, signifying life and growth.

The power of a procession to ritualize meaning should not be underestimated, especially when it includes the bringing in of the coffin. It acts out the coming in and the coming together of the congregation. As a rite of passage and upholding, it focuses the meanings that the larger process of death and resurrection holds for the grieving. It gives physical form to the aspiration of the people toward God. A common and traditional order is (1) processional cross, (2) paschal (Easter) candle or processional candles, (3) presiding pastor, (4) assisting pastors, (5) choir, (6) the coffin carried by pallbearers, (7) the bereaved (if they have not previously been seated), and perhaps (8) official representatives from associations to which the deceased belonged. Children, grandchildren, or other family members may carry flowers, the family Bible, or symbols of the life and work of the deceased. But a procession need not be so elaborate or rigidly ordered. It may be simple, and its very simplicity can be a powerful witness.

It is most helpful, however, to plan the procession carefully. Prior to the procession, the processional cross and paschal candle or processional candles should be in readiness at the point at which the procession is to begin. In both procession and recession, the coffin should be physically carried by the pallbearers as a sign of respect, rather than being rolled in on wheels. Congregations planning or remodeling worship space should provide an aisle six-and-a-half feet or wider to provide room for pallbearers. The pall may be laid over the last pew in readiness for the arrival of the coffin and placed over the coffin before it is brought into the place of worship.

Chancel arrangements should also be planned. The seating of the participants should be explained to them in advance, and provision should also be made for the placing of objects once they have been carried forward in the procession. The processional cross holder should be in its usual place in the chancel, for instance, and the paschal candle holder should be in place at the head of where the coffin will be. Agreement should be made with pallbearers and the funeral director to position the coffin at right angles to the Lord's table, not laterally. It is traditional that the head of the coffin be toward the congregation unless the person was ordained, in which case the head is toward the Lord's table. This suggests the position of laity sitting in the pews and clergy in the chancel. Others today prefer that all coffins be placed with the head toward the Lord's table. If Holy Communion is to be celebrated, however, the coffin may need to be located differently, depending on the architecture and chancel appointments, so that access to the communion rail or to appropriate stations for serving the people is provided. The coffin should remain closed during the service and, except in unusual circumstances, thereafter as well.

The paschal (Easter) candle is a powerful symbol of the gospel, both at funerals and at other times. It stands lighted at a central place in all worship services during the Great Fifty Days of Easter as a symbol of the risen Christ, comparable in the exodus of Christians through the waters of baptism to the pillar of fire in the Exodus of the children of Israel through the Red Sea. At other times of the year, it stands at the font and is lighted at baptism. At funerals it is lighted and stands at the head of the coffin in token of Christ's leading the baptized through the exodus of death and resurrection.

During the procession, a hymn of praise may be sung, or the pastor may say the Word of Grace while preceding the coffin in the procession. In either case, the congregation stands during the procession.

b. The Word of Grace

The Word of Grace is spoken by the pastor either while preceding the coffin in the procession or, if the coffin is in place and there is no procession, from the chancel with the congregation standing. The pastor may choose to speak the opening words from a lower elevation, perhaps near the head of the coffin and nearer to the people.

The phrase "the Word of Grace" is used intentionally to convey several meanings simultaneously. "Word" means God's self-disclosure and self-giving. "Grace" suggests the active reality of God's love in calling, meeting, and dealing with the people. The printed text, taken from John's Gospel and the book of Revelation, is obviously Christ centered, just as grace is. Through the text, Christ's voice opens the service; the words are sayings attributed by believers to Christ. The mysterious presence of Christ is offered. The cosmic meaning of Christ's victory over sin and death is declared. Christ's life is promised now and in the future.

c. Greeting

The greeting states the purpose of the service as praise and proclamation. Within this frame, it also marks in a natural way the human character of the assembly. It realistically recognizes the people's feelings of grief, loss, and pain. Naming the deceased makes the service personal without making it *too* personal.

If a pall was not placed on the coffin during the gathering, the words connected with that act may be spoken immediately after the greeting. While saying these words, the pastor may stand near the head of the coffin, facing the coffin and perhaps extending an arm over it at the sentence, "As in baptism . . . " and then speaking directly to the people the remaining sentences beginning, "Here and now. . . . "

d. Hymn or Song

The location of the opening hymn or song in the service is at the discretion of the pastor. It may come before, during, or after the procession, after the Word of Grace, or after the greeting. A strong congregational hymn on the greatness and goodness of God is most appropriate here.

The term *song* is used here and elsewhere as an alternative to *hymn*. The term is biblical and is meant to suggest that, in general, vocal music is preferable to instrumental. It is less restrictive in meaning than *hymn*, although it certainly includes hymns, and it is especially intended to enlist the participation of the people.

Here and elsewhere in the service, the choice of music is of crucial importance and should be a matter in which pastor, musician, and family all have a voice. Because the character of the music so powerfully affects the character of the whole service, these guidelines are suggested:

1. Music is faith and doctrine experienced in one of their most powerful forms. Great care should be taken with it. Music at the funeral is not to be used as psychological manipulation or soothing syrup. It is to proclaim the gospel and provide for the people's response. Texts in keeping with a Christian view of death and resurrection should be chosen.
2. Music is the servant of the liturgy and should be liturgically evaluated.
3. Because the service is a congregational act and declares the Church's faith, its quality as church music must, therefore, be set beside other considerations, including the wishes of the family. Actually, tension between these need not arise, given sensitive guidance by pastor and musician. In the *Church's* faith, the *individual's* faith is expressed and strengthened.

4. Familiar music is usually best, although on occasion music of Christian integrity and strength—like the gospel itself—may seem to be "over against" the people as well as "for" them. Long-term interpretation and education is needed if the people are to gain "ownership" of unfamiliar or uncongenial music as *their* worship, and a funeral is not the time to impose such music on an unprepared people.

5. Generally, singing by the congregation is preferable, but if there are not enough persons present to enable congregational singing, a song may be played on an instrument or sung as a solo or by a choir.

6. If live music is not possible, and only recorded music is available, music of Christian faith and of strength, well performed, should be selected.

7. Music may be chosen from any period, ancient to contemporary.

8. Music selected should be performed in a manner that exemplifies a Christian understanding of death and resurrection, so that the Easter faith is expressed. All artiness, theatricality, or emotional manipulation should be avoided.

e. Prayer

What constitutes appropriate prayer at this point will be indicated by the circumstances of each particular funeral. At that moment early in the service, what are the spiritual condition and needs of the people present? What kinds of prayer are to be offered later in the service? An overview of the whole service and of all the elements of prayer should be kept in mind. Petition for God's help, thanksgiving for the communion of saints, confession of sin, and assurance of pardon seem especially fitting here, and the prayers given in the text are illustrations of these. Other prayers and other kinds of prayer may be offered. Appropriate prayer forms include a pastoral prayer, a series of collects or other short prayers, or a litany.

This time of prayer may be introduced by the ancient and traditional dialogue, spoken or sung: "The Lord be with you." **"And also with you."** "Let us pray." This both invites and affirms the Lord's presence. It anticipates the prayer that follows as response to the already present Lord and even as, in a sense, inspired by the Lord. It mutually involves pastor and people. It is commonly used in other services as well, not only among United Methodists but also ecumenically; many present may know it by heart.

(1) Prayer for God's help is placed first in this service because it fits the situation of the people and marks the primal reality of all Christian prayer: human finitude and dependence on God, God's vulnerability to our dependence, and God's grace answering to our human need. The Christian consciousness of God is basically forged by the faith that ultimately God is affected by the human cry of need, that God possesses not merely intelligence and will but also pathos. The content of the petition invokes biblical meanings, such as grace, light, life, and love. It thrusts to the heart of the gospel in the great Pauline paradox of death and life in Romans 8 and 14.

(2) Prayer of thanksgiving and intercession for the communion of saints, placed second, contrasts human mortality with God's eternity. Even more, it is prayer of the assembled Christian community, embracing those who pray on earth with those in the church triumphant. Devotion concentrically moves from "saints," understood as "all those who have finished their course in faith," through "those dear to us" to the one whom we call by name. The petitions for peace and perpetual light are widespread in Christian funeral liturgies. The "home not made with hands," although originally referring to the celestial body the Christian puts on at the consummation of all things, is also an apt metaphor for marking the sense of final destiny, the homecoming to which faith looks forward.

(3) The prayer of confession conveys the Christian vision of moral reality, the severity as well as the kindness of God who judges, heals, and saves. This prayer is rightly purgative and is meant to deal with the sense of failure, fear, and guilt that grief often brings. However, it is also salvational. Before the holy God, sin is named in some of its elemental forms. These constitute a kind of death from which God's mercy can deliver into life.

When there is confession, the assurance of pardon is essential. Without it, the gospel as redemption and healing, as death and resurrection, is incompletely proclaimed. While the words of pardon may at times seem rhetorical, actually the pastor is here the agent of a grace able to do abundantly more than we can know or think. Further, the pastor has been called to this function just as all Christians have been called to be priests to one another. Only so can ministry be mutually fulfilled and the Church as Christ's Body be purified and built up. The words of absolution used here consist of Paul's sentences in Romans 8:34 and I Corinthians 15:57, and reference is made again to the fugal theme of death and resurrection.

Any or all of these prayers may be used, and each may be introduced with an appropriate bidding sentence, perhaps followed by a response. Such acts successively regrasp the people's consciousness and redirect their devotion. (1) Before the prayer for God's help, the pastor may say: "Blessed be God by whose great mercy we have been born anew to a living hope through the resurrection of Jesus Christ. In his name let us pray"; and the people may respond, "Hear us, Lord." (2) Before the thanksgiving, the pastor may say: "Let us thank God for all the faithful dead and pray for *(Name)*"; and the people may respond, "Lord, receive *(Name)* into your mercy." (3) Before the confession the pastor may say: "Let us confess our sins unto God"; and the people may respond, "O Lamb of God, who takes away the sins of the world, have mercy upon us." The *kyrie* ("Lord, have mercy. Christ, have mercy. Lord, have mercy.") is appropriate here as elsewhere in the service.

As decisions are made concerning the selection or composition of the prayers, here or later in the service, these guidelines are suggested:

1. The whole service, in a sense, is a prayer and should be conducted accordingly. As its name signifies, a Service of Death and Resurrection deals with the most profound truth of the gospel and the deepest drama in religious experience. Significantly, scripture and tradition speak of this as the "saving mystery." The language and form of the prayers should aim to be worthy of this reality.
2. For most people, prayer is the heart of worship. This is particularly true if we bear in mind that much, if not most, music in worship is prayer. Nothing so deeply meets

people's needs at the funeral or so authentically heals. Indeed, the *funeral service is best thought of as prayer centered* rather than as sermon centered.

3. All the prayers, and all of any single prayer, should be addressed to God (as Trinity or one of the persons of the Trinity). The focus and the thrust are toward Divine Reality at the same time that the prayers grasp and lift up the human condition. Thus, speech about God in the third person is to be avoided. Prayer should address God in the second person as "you" or "thou."

4. Usually, all the essential elements of prayer—praise, thanksgiving, confession and absolution, petition, inter- cession, offering or dedication, commendation, ascription, acclamation—will find place in greater or lesser degree in the funeral—in songs, lessons, and elsewhere, as well as in the prayers. Some of the elements will be explicit, some implicit. The elements of thanksgiving and offering of life, however, are especially to be stressed in the Service of Death and Resurrection.

5. Prayers may be spontaneously offered or prayed from a full text or from notes. In any case, they should be prepared in the pastor's mind and soul, freshly for each occasion.

6. While the pastor will usually prepare and offer the prayers, they are not to be just the pastor's self-expression. Rather, they are to express the church's faith. The pastor represents the whole church and prays as its servant and in its name.

7. Prayers at the service may be original with the pastor and prepared for the occasion, taken from the church's heritage of prayer, express the local or ethnic heritage of the congregation, or they may combine these.

8. Some styles of praying are so essentially oral, rather than literary, that they are better transmitted by hearing and remembering than by reading from the printed page. While printed liturgies cannot effectively include exam- ples of such styles, they have a vital place and importance in congregational worship.

9. Care should be taken in altering the archaic language of traditional prayers not to do violence to their cadence, phrasing, and rhythm.

10. The forms of prayer can vary. (a) The pastoral prayer is one form. (b) A coherent sequence of short sections of prayer is another; these may be prefaced with words of bidding and guidance, such as "Let us offer God our thanksgiving for his Church, the communion of saints." (c) Several collects may be grouped together. (d) There may be a litany in which the people participate responsively. (e) Spontaneous prayers, or concerns to be gathered up in prayer, may be invited from the congregation.

11. While the manner and mood of prayers at the service are usually solemn, the leader should take care that they are not voiced in a morbid fashion.

12. Prayers should be true to the experience of the people, faithful to Christian doctrine, simple and unaffected. Liturgical taste and style vary, but the following values should be kept in mind: a sense of the holy, simplicity, clarity, force, movement, rhythm, cadence, beauty, location of emphasis, sound, word color, image, evocative power, and psychological association.

f. Psalm 130

This psalm and those which follow in the Proclamation and Response are not used as scripture lessons but as prayer and praise. Psalm 130, whether sung or read in chorus, functions here as a scripture song. In its total meaning, it voices the situation of the people before God, recapitulates the drama of death and resurrection, and marks the salvational character of the service. It expresses mercy and judgment, trust and fear, forgiveness and guilt, and the future and the present. As such, it combines redemption and healing. Functionally, it draws together and concludes the Entrance, the first major division of the service, and provides a bridge to the Proclamation and Response. Ever since John Wesley heard it sung on the day of his Aldersgate experience, Psalm 130 has been prominent in Wesleyan tradition.

The version printed in the service is taken, with modifications, from the King James Version of the Bible because of its intrinsic power and beauty. Other versions, as well as other psalms, could be used.

2. Proclamation and Response

a. Scripture and Praise

The entire Service of Death and Resurrection is in one sense proclamation. As with all Christian worship, the test both of the whole and of the parts is whether the service is kerygmatic—that is, whether the gospel is proclaimed in a way that ministers to people. Of course, no single service and no single part can adequately do this, but surely the funeral must embody the gospel as fully and faithfully as possible. Thus a funeral is no place for the peripheral or trivial or merely sentimental, and the fatefulness of the experience of death must be matched with the fatefulness of the gospel. In this section, proclamation is forthrightly named and centered in scripture and sermon.

Although the service makes no mention of a prayer for illumination, such as is found in the Sunday Service of Word and Table, such a prayer may be used before the first scripture reading to ask the Spirit's aid in the proclamation, in the hearing, and in the understanding of God's Word. It can signal that human speaking and hearing are at the service of a Reality other and greater than the reader or preacher and can mark the people's, as well as the pastor's, duty both to hear and to speak the Word. However, since Psalm 130 fulfills this function with such solemnity and power, and since the very gravity of the funeral occasion itself communicates a sense of waiting upon God, the prayer for illumination can appropriately be omitted.

The arrangement of scripture readings follows the traditional sequence in Christian worship of Old Testament lesson, New Testament lesson, and Gospel. Readings should not be a hodgepodge; rather, they should be selected to embody the integrity and fullness of the gospel and to culminate in words attributed to Jesus himself in the Gospels. This principle governs the choice of "preferred" and "recommended" lessons and gives them unity, sequence, and dramatic movement.

Isaiah 40 and its recommended alternatives strongly proclaim the Old Testament meanings of death and resurrection. In the New Testament, I Corinthians 15 forthrightly proclaims the theme of death and resurrection with reason and passion: "First and foremost, I handed on to you the facts . . . that Christ died . . . was buried . . . was raised . . . and appeared . . ." (vv. 3-5 NEB). Here death and resurrection are unequivocally declared as historical event and then interpreted. Thus this epistle appropriately precedes the soaring passages of Revelation 21 and 22: "the new heaven," "the new earth," "the holy city." The recommended alternatives likewise proclaim death and resurrection. These readings culminate in the great assurance of John 14 ("Let not your hearts be troubled. . . . I am the way. . . . Because I live, you will live also. . . .") and its recommended alternatives.

Readings from Christian scripture are essential in all funeral services conducted by a Christian minister; it is hard to think of a situation where this would not be the case. If nonscriptural readings are used, they should supplement, not displace, scripture. A good way to incorporate such readings or poems is at the time of witness following the sermon.

Particular situations may require particular readings appropriate to them. Certainly readings other than those listed may be used. Closer scrutiny, however, may reveal that the customary readings fit the situation better than may first have been supposed.

Readings may be chosen from any Bible version of integrity and good liturgical quality. Various versions should be consulted and compared. When passages are spliced together or condensed, essential meaning should be preserved. Punctuation may be changed, although not irresponsibly, to facilitate flow of meaning. Occasionally, different translations using both ancient and modern forms may be fused together if this serves liturgical purpose. The clarity of modern translations is always important, but in good worship translational accuracy is not the maximum value. Certain verbal usages in more traditional versions, while not as "modern" as we might wish, often have a landmark quality that can hardly be changed without impoverishment.

The place, means, manner, and posture of reading and hearing are important. These symbolically convey—or fail to convey—vital meanings that are really an acted-out commentary on the gospel. They are not empty ceremony; in their way, they too proclaim. While lessons may be read from pulpit or lectern or from the midst of the people, there is much to be said for reading them from the place from which the sermon is to be preached.

This underscores the basis of preaching in scripture. The same reasons that may lead a congregation to stand for the reading of the gospel in the Sunday service can lead them to stand for its reading at funerals. The physical character and appearance of the Bible—the way it is carried and handled, and even opened—are as important at a funeral as in the Sunday service. The use, especially in a funeral home, of the Bible normally used in a congregation's services communicates a sense of the sacredness of the Word and a feeling for church and tradition better than does reading from a leaflet or small service book. The phrases used to introduce the readings in the Sunday service can likewise be used at funerals.

Lessons may be read by others than the pastor. In fact, reading by members of the family or friends of the deceased should be encouraged but with sensitivity to those who feel hesitant to do this or for whom it may be emotionally too difficult. Who can know what such an action may mean for those who read and for those who hear, at the moment itself or in days to come?

The use of Psalm 23 between Old and New Testament lessons is felt to be virtually essential. It is not a lesson; it is prayer and praise. Preferably, it should be sung—or, if necessary, spoken—by the people. Several suitable sung or spoken settings are found in the hymnal. If it is read, there is much to be said for using the familiar King James Version, which so many people have memorized and which makes references to death and life after death in a way that most modern translations do not. This psalm has also since ancient times been associated by Christians with Holy Communion and takes on a special meaning when the Service of Death and Resurrection includes communion. In unusual circumstances, one of the other recommended psalms may be substituted.

Between the New Testament lesson and the Gospel there may be a psalm or hymn. Just as the rhythm of call and response is served by interspersing reading with praise, so also is the people's sense of time and movement. A sequence of three or four passages of scripture, plus sermon, without interruption, may simply be too many words, and the people's attention may lag. The length of passages, of course, needs to be borne in mind. Yet, clock time here is not so important as the people's sense of liturgical and psychological time.

As a general rule, music at this point should be sung by the people, be organic to the movement of the service, and be theologically consistent with the gospel of death and resurrection. It should not clash with the surrounding scripture readings. At the same time, all music is evocative, and the dynamic meanings it suggests may proclaim the gospel more effectively than the rational content of the musical text would lead one to expect.

b. Sermon, Naming, and Witness

A funeral is no place for a long sermon. The sermon, though brief, should be primarily a proclamation of the gospel of Jesus Christ. It is not a eulogy or an impressionistic meditation, not a moral or theological lecture, not manufactured inspiration or psychological therapy. But while the sermon is proclamatory, it is not a one-way thunderbolt. It is to be verified by its ministering quality. It is human speech through which Christ the Word tenderly, truthfully, and healingly engages the souls of the people where they are, in their hurt and need. It is a verbal means of grace, potentially as sacramental and sacrificial as the bread and wine of Holy Communion, that God's Spirit may use to raise people into newness of life. And it anticipates the people's response in the offering of their lives that follows.

While the sermon should not be primarily a eulogy, the particular death and the particular grief of the occasion need to be recognized in their human character. The sermon should not be so depersonalized that reference to the deceased and the mourners is eliminated. If some funerals are too personalized, others are too impersonal. The pastor will need to walk a liturgical fine line here as well as throughout the service. Each sermon should be sensitively and freshly prepared for the particular occasion. While the pastor does the preparing, however, it is God's Word and the Church's faith that speak.

The sermon may lead into, or include, acts of *naming* and *witness*, and these may help in making the proclamation all that it should be. The optional act of *naming* is intended to keep proclamation related to the real situation of the people in a ministering way. The life and death of the deceased may be gathered up by the reading of a memorial or appropriate statement, or in other ways, by the pastor or others. The purpose is to personalize the service by singling out and lifting up the individual, human selfhood of the deceased, and by identifying— implicitly or explicitly—the relationships of the deceased to the mourners. It may be a natural part of, or immediately follow, the sermon. It may be used separately or joined to the act of witness that follows. An appropriate memorial or obituary-type statement may be prepared in advance and read by the pastor or someone else, or signs and symbols described below under Witness may be used. Such an act locates the deceased in the communities—geographical, familial, religious, educational, social, vocational—that significantly shaped his or her life. The act can recognize particular achievements. It can be a means of summarily reviewing and cherishing the life of the deceased, and then of letting go, reinforcing the finality of death even while evoking marvel before the color and individuality of human life. For a Christian, it declares again the name connected with baptism, when the deceased was symbolically buried and raised with Christ and grafted as an individual member into his Body, the Church. Naming can also be done in other ways—elsewhere in this service, at the services on the Sunday following the funeral, on All Saints, and at a wide variety of memorial and commemorative services.

In optional acts of *witness*, family, friends, and members of the congregation may briefly voice their thankfulness to God for the grace they have received in the life of the deceased and in their Christian faith and joy. Signs of faith, hope, and love may be exchanged. These acts are intended to direct thought to the deceased, but within the context of God's grace. This context is vital. The value of personalizing the service in a natural human way is retained, but the personalizing is set within these larger meanings that constitute a form of proclamation. The term *witness* should be carefully noted because it includes the *purpose*, as well as the *name*, of these acts of proclamation and can, therefore, caution participants against lapsing into dishonest eulogy with all its dangers.

As a matter of fact, the nature and function of eulogy may need to be rethought. If there is dishonest eulogy, there is also truthful and appropriate eulogy. Understood as "tribute" or "appreciation," eulogy can be thankfulness, and surely thankfulness to God—even when verbally addressed to people—is not out of place in proclamation. Further, the qualities of the personality and life of the deceased for which thanks is given can be seen as having "graced" the lives of the survivors. This does not mean, of course, that the deceased is falsely idealized. Rather, all that is appreciated is gratefully acknowledged as a gift from God. Those invited to offer witness should have this explained to them in advance.

The emotional poignancy of this action, like that of naming, involves risk, but risks may be taken. Psychologically, the expression of feelings is important. Theologically, such signs as words, objects, and gestures enable people to act out before God and with one another their thanksgiving, faith, hope, love, and joy.

There are many forms of witness, each with its distinctive sign values: (1) The brief *verbal tribute*, preferably arranged for and prepared in advance. (2) The traditional *Peace*—verbal exchange, handclasp, silent embrace. (3) The bringing in or placing of *flowers*, perhaps of the kind most loved by the deceased. (4) Brief *readings* from favorite books or poems. (5) Display of favorite *pictures*. (6) *Symbols* of the vocation or accomplishments of the deceased—a tool, a garment, an award, a product of the deceased's work. (7) Reading of selected *messages and tributes* from mourners unable to be present. (8) Recognition of people who have traveled from a considerable distance, since their *travel* is itself a witness. (9) Silently laying on the coffin *a sheaf of wheat*, whose grain must fall into the ground and die before it can bring forth life. (10) When appropriate, the *death mask* of the deceased. Imagination and faith may suggest other signs.

The pastor may incorporate in the announcement of this time of witness the words of Paul:

> Praise be to the God and Father of our Lord Jesus Christ, the all-merciful Father, the God whose consolation never fails us! He comforts us in all our troubles, so that we in turn may be able to comfort others in any trouble of theirs and to share with them the consolation we ourselves receive from God. (II Corinthians 1:3-4 NEB)

In some situations, it may be better to separate this time of witness from the funeral itself and incorporate it into an informal service of prayer and thanksgiving before or after the funeral. Such acts of witness may also be used, with appropriate modifications, at memorial services or other occasions.

c. Response to the Word

Two congregational responses are suggested following the proclamation of the gospel in the above acts. In these responses, the people offer their trust in God's saving action in Jesus Christ as the event on which they take their stand and by which they are prepared to live and die.

A congregational *hymn or song* of faith is an appropriate response to the gospel message that has been heard. Many persons and congregations express their faith and trust more fully by singing than by speaking.

The Apostles' Creed may be said by the congregation, standing, either before or after or instead of the hymn or song. It has a special set of meanings at a Service of Death and Resurrection. It should be understood as a celebration of salvation events more than as a statement of doctrine. Originally, all the professions of faith in the New Testament bore this character. They were expressions of joy in the lordship of Christ known through the Jesus of history, doxological rather than didactic. Only later, largely in response to controversy, did creeds come to be seen as statements of dogma. As the worshipers' response to proclamation, the creed is a reoffering of heart and mind. It recalls the fact of our baptism and the reality of our baptismal covenant and faith. It singles out and avows the death and resurrection of Jesus Christ as decisive for our destiny.

These responses are optional. It is recognized that there are funerals in which this service may be used and in which the character of the gathering is such that a corporate expression of Christian faith would be impossible, or at least lack integrity. In such a case, where the witness to the gospel has been made, but where only a fraction of those present could honestly respond in faith, it may be best to omit the response or to have a musical response of faith offered by a soloist or a small ensemble.

A note of caution is in order, however. Because funeral congregations so commonly include persons other than committed Christians, it is easy to rationalize a pattern of omitting congregational acts of faith. It is important to remember all the persons present who want and need the opportunity to express their faith and to remember that those present who cannot with integrity do so can quietly refrain from singing or speaking.

3. The Commendation

All that has gone before in this service leads up in a natural movement and momentum to *the commendation*, which refers to the God of Jesus Christ as the end beyond all other ends unto whom we live and die; to faith's insight that our human destiny is in this God; and to a liturgical act that declares this faith. This time of prayer reflects the conviction that the whole service is best thought of as prayer centered rather than as sermon centered. This time might also be called "the offering of life." If the commital service normally used at the grave or cremation is to conclude this service, it may be shortened and substituted for the commendation. Since, however, the committal should whenever possible be conducted at the burial site and often cannot be held immediately following the funeral, and since many who attend the funeral may not attend the committal, a committal *outside of* this service is no substitute for the commendation *within* this service.

Several understandings should be made clear. Of course, response in the form of commendation or offering occurs throughout the service and in acts within acts. Neither the funeral nor Christian worship in general should ever be designed to produce spiritual states or psychological experiences at prescribed moments. Who can ever say where the offering of life really occurs or what form it will take? Yet, provision for offering of life needs to be intentional and definite. Without it, worship is not complete and the proclamation of the gospel as death and resurrection is not fulfilled.

Worshipers may or may not perceive the depth of meaning commendation holds at the time it is performed or its implications for their existence. Outwardly, commendation may appear to be an action willed and performed by the people themselves. Essentially and inwardly, however, it is caused by the action of God. It is response to divine grace already active in conscious and unconscious levels of personality. It is God acting in, with, and under the outward forms of human action. In this deep sense, the worshiper's offering or committal of life is really God's raising to life. Nothing less than resurrection can come to pass. Encounter with death becomes transformed into an experience of newness of life now for the living, identifying marks of which are often the breaking of the grip of guilt and fear, a sense of healing, greater sensitivity, a saner vision of reality, a longer view of time that can even become a sense of eternity, a renewal of willed obedience, a peace that passes understanding. In short, through the commendation or offering of life as a union with God for one's destiny, the self is reconstituted. This union alone matches the fatefulness of our human experience of death.

One or more prayers may be offered. Three such prayers are printed in the text, the first of which is basically intercession and the second and third of which are basically commendation. Other prayers may be used. They may take the form of a pastoral prayer, a series of shorter prayers, or a litany. These prayers offer to God the life of the deceased and the life of the people. The people present themselves as a holy and living sacrifice to God. The result for them can be an experience of destiny, a coming home, or a restoration of life.

Intercession is a natural part of the act of commendation. Intercessory prayer is probably as tender and bold an act of love as there is. By its very nature, it is intensely mutual. It rightly enlists sympathy and taxes sensitivity and imagination. Here the true needs of those who mourn, not merely superficial needs, are apprehended and named—needs such as light, strength, forgiveness, peace, and love. Intercession is also a bold act of faith; probably there is none bolder. Trust in God's nature as active love is audaciously put forth. Intercession is also the Church functioning as Church; it has been "called out" for just this purpose. The priesthood of all believers is here experienced and declared. In intercession, the prayer of the Church on earth mystically joins with the praise and prayer of the Church in heaven.

The two prayers of commendation serve several purposes. They are forthright offerings to God of the deceased through word, metaphor, and gesture. They are meant to communicate a sense of finality and termination and to be a final act of love. They acknowledge our beginning and our end in the God revealed to us in Jesus Christ. They describe resurrection as God's raising us, not as our raising of ourselves. They link the offering of the life of the survivors with the act of the offering of the deceased. They invoke the first and greatest commandment as the condition of the new life into which God raises his people. They express the Christian hope of joy in God's kingdom after death. They suggest the spirit of what has been called the Christian prayer beyond all prayers: Jesus' final words, "Father, into thy hands I commend my spirit." The laying of hands on the coffin adds the dimension of "body language" to our commendation.

These prayers may need to be rethought for services for the unchurched or non-Christian. The assumptions of faith underlying these prayers may not apply. On the other hand, these prayers may be more appropriate than might at first be supposed. Pastoral sensitivity is of crucial importance here.

4. *Thanksgiving and Communion*

a. If Holy Communion Is Not Celebrated

If Holy Communion is not to be celebrated, the service continues with the prayer of thansgiving given in the text, followed by the Lord's Prayer, an appropriate hymn, and the Dismissal with Blessing.

(1) *Thanksgiving or doxology* is fittingly the first and last word in Christian prayer. In this setting, prayer praises God for his love in creation and in redemption as the reality on which faith takes it ultimate stand. Thanksgiving for this love frames everything else, even suffering and sorrow.

(2) *The Lord's Prayer* prayed in unison appropriately concludes this part of the service. It gathers up all other prayers and is probably the most universal bond of Christian faith. Its final

ascription of power and glory, ending with the word *forever,* seals all else with a doxology of invincible faith and joy.

(3) *The concluding hymn* should, if possible, be sung by the congregation. The Doxology ("Praise God from Whom All Blessings Flow") would be an appropriate choice and is well enough known that many will sing it from memory.

b. If Holy Communion Is Celebrated

Provision for Holy Communion at a funeral may seem strange to most United Methodists. In congregations in which such celebrations would be perceived as so incongruous as to be disabling, they should not be conducted. Neither should Holy Communion be celebrated at a funeral for the unchurched or the non-Christian. Only after consultation with the family of the deceased, or with the deceased before death, and in accord with the congregation's guidelines for worship, should communion be celebrated. Here the meanings—true or incomplete or distorted—that communion has come to hold for people across the years need to be pastorally discerned and weighed alongside liturgical and theological integrity.

In educating the people and deciding the question, it should be borne in mind that, from the Church's beginning, the Eucharist (Holy Communion) was probably celebrated by the congregation at the time of a Christian's death. From the third century on, it was celebrated both at the grave and in congregational assembly. Probably the original impulse was the natural wish of the living to maintain union with departed relatives and friends, Holy Communion being the deepest expression of that union. Union of the faithful was in and through Christ—not, as so often thought today, even by church people, through spiritualist contact with the dead. Later, the purpose of the funeral Eucharist changed and became more propritiatory, issuing in the corruptions against which the leaders of the Reformation protested. In our ecumenical age, these controversies have largely been resolved, and appreciation of the common sacramental heritage that predated them has grown to embrace celebration of the funeral Eucharist.

This appreciation is, of course, part of the movement toward restoring the full, ancient unity of the Service of Word and Table as normative for a congregation's life. The question becomes, then, "Are not both Word and Table similarly desirable at the funeral if the gospel is to be proclaimed in its fullness?"

It should be remembered that Holy Communion is proclamation of the gospel message of death and resurrection *par excellence* with all its overtones of penitence and faith or brokenness and healing or sorrow and joy. In this sense, Holy Communion is as evangelical—indeed, as evangelistic—an act as the church performs. Response to the message of death and resurrection is inevitably the thankful offering and reoffering by the people of their lives, their being taken up into Jesus' destiny as their own, their sense of oneness with all who through him have lived and died, their nourishment with his bread and wine for the burdens they bear, and the taking up of Jesus' cross as their way to life. Worship in the character of Holy Meal here represents better than it does anywhere else the supper Jesus ate with his disciples the night before his death. It recalls further the meals Jesus ate with his disciples at which he disclosed his risen life. It is a foretaste of the supper of the Lamb, which Jesus promised to eat with his own in the day of his kingdom. It is "the communion of saints"—our communion here and now at the Lord's table with the family of Christ "at all times and in all places," living and dead, on earth and in heaven.

The Order for Holy Communion on pages 85-87 of *The Book of Services* follows the same pattern as does Holy Communion in the Service of Word and Table, but with words designed to be appropriate to a Service of Death and Resurrection. The understandings and suggestions for Holy Communion, given in Part I of this book, can be applied to the funeral or memorial occasion. Family members and friends of the deceased may bring the bread and wine to the Lord's table either in an opening procession or at the beginning of the Order for Holy Communion itself, and they may later assist in the distribution of communion. Since there are likely to be persons present who choose not to receive communion, particular sensitivity should be exercised not to usher the congregation forward in such a way as to make such persons feel conspicuous or do anything else that would cause them to feel pressure or embarrassment. It is appropriate that there be a doxology or other hymn of praise and thanksgiving after the communion.

Alternatively, Holy Communion may be celebrated before a common meal following the Service or with the family at some time following the Service. In such a case, it can be regarded as a continuation of the Service, and nothing need be repeated. Of course, the pastor would preside at such a celebration just as at the Service itself.

5. Dismissal with Blessing

The term *dismissal* means "sending" and rightly incorporates into the Service of Death and Resurrection the congregation's missional nature. The congregation has been gathered as those who have been sent, and they are sent forth as those who have been gathered. The death and resurrection theme of the service is the same theme the Christian is to live out in the world, and service to God in assembly for worship continues in service to people everywhere. While it may seem odd to send people forth in mission at the very time when as mourners they are likely to feel most weak, passive, and "in shock," the fact is that those very people at that very moment are being sent forth on a very demanding part of their Christian mission—namely, continuing in the days and weeks ahead to uphold and to minister to one another in their common grief and mourning. To be strengthened for these tasks, they surely need God's blessing.

The term *blessing* has more of the meaning of "sealing." The people bless God, but even more they are blessed by God—that is, they are once more marked as God's, established in God, covered with God's grace, and held in God's peace.

The scriptural and traditional benedictions printed in the text convey these two meanings, dismissal and blessing, and are the fitting conclusion to a service as intensely Christian as the Service of Death and Resurrection. They should be spoken by the pastor face-to-face with the standing congregation, not from the rear of the church.

If the concluding hymn is a recessional, it follows, rather than precedes, the dismissal with blessing. The recession may form and proceed in approximately the same order as the procession.

If there is no recession, the pastor may take up a position before the coffin and precede it as it is borne from the place of the service to the hearse, again carried by pallbearers. The pastor should consult with the funeral director before the funeral about procedures at this point.

There may be music during the departure of the people, but there is much to be aid for not having music here and instead concluding the service in silence.

6. An Order of Committal

The word *committal* in the title of this service holds several meanings and has already been discussed above on pages 130-33. Functionally, it refers to the disposition of the body of the deceased. Sociologically, it denotes a communal act of respect and homage to the deceased. Psychologically, it implies a facing of the fact of death and a final letting go. Theologically, it reflects the Christian vision of things seen and unseen. Here the people give thanks to God for the deceased and pray for the dead and the living. Especially here the people offer to God the life of the deceased and their own lives. All these meanings mingle liturgically, and the Committal becomes a service of confrontation with destiny. Thus understood, the Committal service recapitulates some of the meanings of the Service of Death and Resurrection, particularly the Commendation.

If it is held at a considerable distance of time or place from the funeral service, pastoral judgment will determine how long the committal service should be and what it should include. Generally, committal services are too brief, especially when an interval has elapsed between funeral and committal and when numbers of people attend the committal who were not present at the funeral. Options in this committal service enable it to be expanded.

Sometimes it is necessary to include the Committal as part of the funeral service. If so, the order should be shortened as provided for and substituted for the Commendation, as was discussed above. If military, civic, or fraternal rites are conducted, they should follow the committal service.

Clearly, the poignancy of this moment calls for great sensitivity, both liturgically and pastorally. The very variety of occasions of committal—burial of the body or its ashes in the ground, entombment above ground, burial at sea, donation of the body for medical purposes, and scattering of ashes—underscores this need. This order is intended primarily for burial in the ground. However, it can be adapted for cremation or the interment of ashes, for burial above ground or at sea, or when the body is donated for medical purposes.

Thus the rubric, "The pastor should preside," holds particular significance. Others may participate in conducting the service, and of course the wishes of the family, as well as local custom and tradition, should be borne in mind. The fatefulness with which liturgy is charged at this moment, however, is too great for the service to be determined by other than a pastor—ordained or unordained—responsible for acting in the name of Christ and the Church. Only in cases of genuine necessity or of careful choice should anyone other than the pastor who conducted the funeral service preside at the committal service.

An important part of the pastor's responsibility is to take particular care with ceremony and symbol because they hold such deep religious meaning here. Indeed, they will likely speak more powerfully than words. Spiritual intention, honesty, simplicity, naturalness—these are the criteria to go by. Because of the significance of ceremony and symbol, the pastor in charge should come to a clear understanding in advance with the funeral director concerning all parts of the ceremony.

a. Gathering

In most situations, the people will *gather* informally at the grave. Since the surrounding space, weather, numbers in attendance, and custom affect the physical movement of the people, the manner of gathering and the arrangement of the assembly may need to be worked out with care and adaptability. Possibly an informal procession of all the people—led by the pastor, followed by the pallbearers carrying the coffin and then by the family—may voice Christian meaning better than detaining the people until the coffin is in place.

Too smooth or self-conscious or furtive attempts to lessen the starkness of the occasion, while usually well meant, are false. The very earthiness, even unexpected awkwardness, of physical movement in procession and in carrying and placing the coffin can contribute honesty and reality to the moment. The people, likewise, need not be herded into rows; an informal circle around the grave, for example, may better express Christian meaning. The pastor should stand at the head of the grave and of the unlowered coffin.

b. Opening Sentences

One or more of the *opening sentences* in the text may be spoken. They embody a sequence of devotion that contrapuntally voices the gospel of death and resurrection. They include a portion of a ninth-century antiphon used in the Episcopal *Book of Common Prayer*, Psalm 124:8, Romans 8:11, selected verses from I Corinthians 15, and Psalm 16:9, 11. They should be spoken to the people loudly enough to be heard.

c. Opening Prayer

The *prayer* that follows is revised from traditional sources and links the acts of committal of the deceased with the self-offering of the people.

d. Scripture

The *scripture readings* (I Peter 1:3-9 and John 12:24-26) are optional. They proclaim the gospel promise of resurrection, but not without qualification; faith and obedience still are undertones.

e. The Committal

The *committal* is action accompanied by words. The pastor at this moment faces the coffin—not necessarily the people—turning if need be to do so.

The sentences of committal open with Jesus' prayer of committal from the cross, name the deceased by Christian (or first) name, and include elements from the Church's traditional liturgies. The concluding sentences are from Revelation 14:13. As indicated, alternative words are to be used when the body is not in fact being committed to "the ground." The words *the elements* are appropriate at cremation, and the words *its resting place* are appropriate when that resting place is not in the ground.

It is desirable that the coffin be lowered at this point in the service, if possible beginning at the words, "This body we commit to the ground." Less preferably, the coffin may be lowered immediately after the people have gathered or immediately after the final blessing. In any case, it seriously compromises the integrity and symbolic power of the service to wait and lower the coffin surreptitiously after the mourners have left.

If possible, real earth from the grave—not flowers, or sand from envelopes—should be cast on the coffin by the pastor, not by the funeral director. Simultaneously, earth may be cast on the coffin by family members or by other mourners if desired. Earth or flowers may be dropped onto the lowered coffin after the final blessing as a symbol of respect, committal, and farewell by other mourners if desired. Arrangements for gesture and symbol here should be planned in advance with the funeral director and family, although spontaneous expressions should not be ruled out.

f. Closing Prayers

The choice of *prayers* after the Committal depends on the needs of the people, on the desired length of the service, on whether the committal service is held separately from the funeral service or included in it, and on the pastor's liturgical instinct and sensitivity. Other prayers than those printed may, of course, be used. Prayers from the concluding section of the Service of Death and Resurrection may also be used. Extemporary prayer by the pastor may also be appropriate. The first four prayers in the text are largely revisions taken from the Church's traditional liturgies. They include thanksgiving, intercession for the deceased and the mourners, and petition for God's grace, and they constitute a unity. The last prayer combines these elements. Places in the prayers where the first name of the deceased is spoken and where masculine or feminine pronouns need to be inserted should be noted. The people respond with the "Amen." The Lord's prayer may follow.

g. Hymn or Song

The option of a *hymn or song* should be considered if it is judged that the service will not be unduly prolonged and if music here is not emotionally overwhelming. Although the people will not have hymnals, sometimes one or two stanzas of a familiar hymn, or a familiar doxology or chorus, can be sung from memory.

h. Dismissal with Blessing

The *blessing* (Jude 24) stresses the character of God as able to guard the Christian amid frailty and vicissitude until the day of Christ's coming. As ascription and doxology, it also offers the entire service as an act of worship to God. The text is taken mainly from the King James Version because of its poetic quality.

The pastor faces the people in giving the blessing, using whatever gesture is felt to be liturgically appropriate, perhaps signing the people with the Christian sign of the cross. Then, usually, though not always, the pastor's physical movement should signal a definite conclusion to the service, probably by approaching relatives or other mourners in quiet farewell or by accompanying them as they leave. On occasion, however, if the emotional intensity is not too great and if weather and other circumstances permit, pastor and people may wish to tarry and to greet and visit with one another in a natural way.

NOTES

Chapter I: Services of Word and Table

1. *John Wesley's Sunday Service of the Methodists in North America*, with an introduction by James F. White [A Methodist Bicentennial Commemorative Reprint from *Quarterly Review*] (Nashville: The United Methodist Publishing House and the United Methodist Board of Higher Education and Ministry, 1984), p. iii (cf. Galatians 5:1).
2. *Ibid.*, p. ii.
3. Albert C. Outler, ed., *The Works of John Wesley*, vol. 3 (Sermons III)(Nashville: Abingdon Press, 1986), Sermon 101, pp. 427ff.
4. John C. Bowmer, *The Sacrament of the Lord's Supper in Early Methodism* (London: Dacre Press, 1951), pp. 49 ff.
5. Nolan B. Harmon, *The Rites and Ritual of Episcopal Methodism* (Nashville: Publishing House of The M. E. Church, South, 1926), pp. 86ff.
6. *The Doctrines and Discipline of the Methodist Episcopal Church* 1792, part I, section XXIII, pp. 40f.
7. *Ibid.*, 1864, p. 41.
8. *The Doctrines and Discipline of the Methodist Episcopal Church, South* 1870, chapter V, section 1, pp. 106ff.
9. *The Methodist Hymnal* (New York: The Methodist Book Concern, 1905).
10. See note 3.
11. *The Book of Hymns* 332, stanza 4.

Chapter IV: A Service of Christian Marriage

1. Horton Davies, *Worship and Theology in England: From Watts and Wesley to Maurice, 1690-1850* (Princeton: Princeton University Press, 1961), p. 137.
2. *A Report by the Liturgical Commission of the General Synod of the Church of England*, "The Wedding Service" (London: SPCK [Central Board of Finance, Church of England], 1975), p. 5.
3. *The First and Second Prayer Books of Edward VI*, introduction by E. C. S. Gibson (London, 1960 reprint).
4. *Spiritual Director's Manual* (Dallas: National Secretariat of the Cursillo Movement, 1976), p. 86.

5. *Prayer Books of Edward VI: A Report by the Liturgical Commission.*
6. *Spiritual Director's Manual.*
7. John Demos, *A Little Commonwealth* (London: Oxford University Press, 1970).
8. See Paul W. Hoon, "The Order for the Service of Marriage" in *Companion to the Book of Worship,* W. F. Dunkle, Jr. and J. D. Quillian, Jr., eds. (Nashville: Abingdon Press, 1970). Entries in "Marriage" in *Oxford Classical Dictionary,* N. S. L. Hammond and H. H. Scullard, eds. (London: Oxford University Press, 1972).
9. H. Richard Niebuhr, *Christ and Culture* (New York: Harper and Brothers, 1951).
10. *Report of the Liturgical Commission,* p. 6.
11. "Naming" in *Ritual in a New Day: An Invitation* (Nashville: Abingdon Press, 1976).